ALL STAR ENGLISH

AN INTEGRATED ESL CURRICULUM

**Charles Skidmore ★ Anne Marie Drayton
Patricia Richard-Amato**

Addison-Wesley Publishing Company

CONTENTS

Featuring:

Reading Skills: Comprehension 10,13, 25, 44, 45, 46, 72, 85, 107, 109, 110, 112 • Reading for a purpose 11,12, 27, 29, 32, 33, 50, 51, 54 • Distinguishing true-false statements 26, 46, 72, 106 • Following directions 35, 42 • Summarizing 46, 66, 84 • Sequencing 45 • Recalling details 67 • Categorizing 68, 105

Writing Skills: Process writing 11, 13, 14, 16–17, 18, 27, 30, 32, 33, 36–37, 38, 56–57, 58, 66, 76–77, 78, 84, 96–97, 98, 116–117, 118 • Letter writing 18, 38, 58, 78, 98, 118 • Note-taking 19, 87, 89, 94 • Creative writing 47, 67, 69 • Guided writing 65

• Using a chart 10, 13, 25, 30, 48, 59, 72, 74, 84, 85, 87, 88, 95, 105, 106, 113, 115

Grammar: Vocabulary development 6, 8, 14, 52, 73, 104, 109, 110 • Using adjectives 6 • Prepositions 28 • Describing quantity 29, 30 • Verb forms 68, 69 • Pronouns 90 • Antecedents 91 • Analogies 104 • Present conditional tense 108

Content Skills: Math 31, 34, 35, 49, 50, 53 • Science 19, 39, 59, 79, 99, 109, 119 • Social Studies 14, 93

A Publication of the World Language Division

Director of Product Development: Judith M. Bittinger

Executive Editor: Elinor Chamas

Editorial Development: Laura M. Alavosus

Text and Cover Design: Taurins Design Associates

Art Direction and Production: Taurins Design Associates

Production and Manufacturing: James W. Gibbons

Illustrators: Denny Bond 89; Len Ebert 3, 23, 43, 63, 83, 103; Tuko Fujisaki 6, 27, 49, 70; Susan Miller 11, 51, 73, 122; Chris Reed 9, 28, 31, 34,35, 42, 50, 52, 104, 105; Dave Sullivan 19, 21, 39, 59, 61, 79, 81, 99, 101, 119, 121.

ISBN 0-201-88089-X
3 4 5 6 7 8 9 10 -CRS- 00 99 98 97

Look at the pictures. Tell what you see. Write about the pictures.

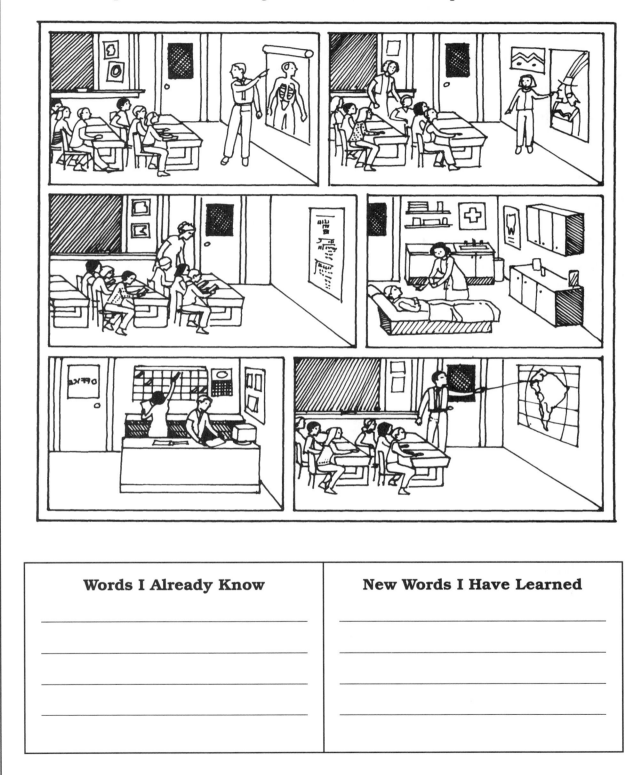

Words I Already Know	**New Words I Have Learned**
_____	_____
_____	_____
_____	_____
_____	_____

(Supports Student Book 2, page 3) **Activating prior knowledge; self-assessment.** Students write the words they know before the lesson begins, then the words they have learned at the end of the lesson. You may want to save this page in students' **Assessment Portfolios.**

Reread the story on pages 4–6 in your student book. Find the information for Carmen. Put it in the chart. Then add information about yourself.

	Carmen	**You**
First name		
Last name		
Country		
Age		
Hair		
Eyes		
Name of best friend		
Favorite things to do		

Now put all the information in this diagram.

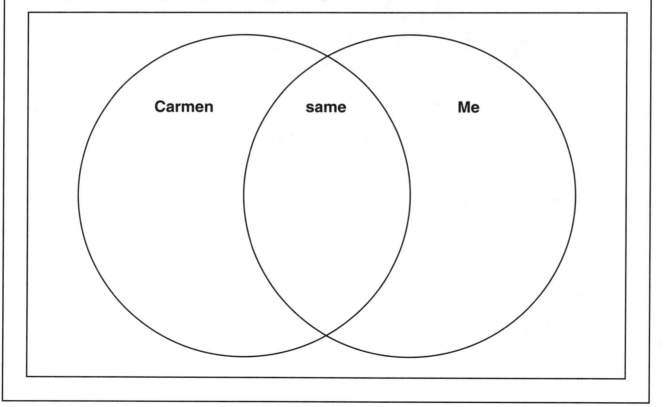

(Supports Student Book 2, pages 4–6) **Data collection; providing information about self; comparing/contrasting.** Before students begin this page, reread aloud, or play the tape of, the student book pages so students can hear the information again. Then have them work independently.

Complete the blanks to write an informational paragraph about yourself.

My name is _____. I am from _____.

I am _____ years old. My hair is _____.

My eyes are _____. My favorite color is _____.

I like to wear _____. My best friend's name is _____.

We like to _____ together.

Reread Hi, My Name is Carmen *in your student book. Complete the paragraph about Carmen.*

I read a story about Carmen Ortiz. _____ is from Puerto

Rico. She is _____ years old. _____ hair is

_____. _____ eyes are _____.

_____ favorite color is _____. She likes to wear

_____ red _____. Her best friend's name is

_____. They like to _____ together.

Read and answer the questions.

1. Where is Carmen from?_____

2. How old is Carmen? _____

3. What color is Carmen's hair? _____

4. What color are Carmen's eyes? _____

5. What is Carmen's favorite color? _____

6. What does Carmen like to wear? _____

7. Who is Carolina? _____

8. What things do Carolina and Carmen like to do? _____

(Supports Student Book 2, pages 4–6) **Practicing key vocabulary; cloze exercise.** Students complete exercises independently. Encourage students to refer to their graphic organizers. You may want to save this page in students' **Assessment Portfolios.**

*Look at the pictures. Use the words in the Data Bank to describe
these friends from outer space.*

Examples: His name is Grom.　　Her name is Bonin.
He is muscular.　　She has long hair.
He is bald.

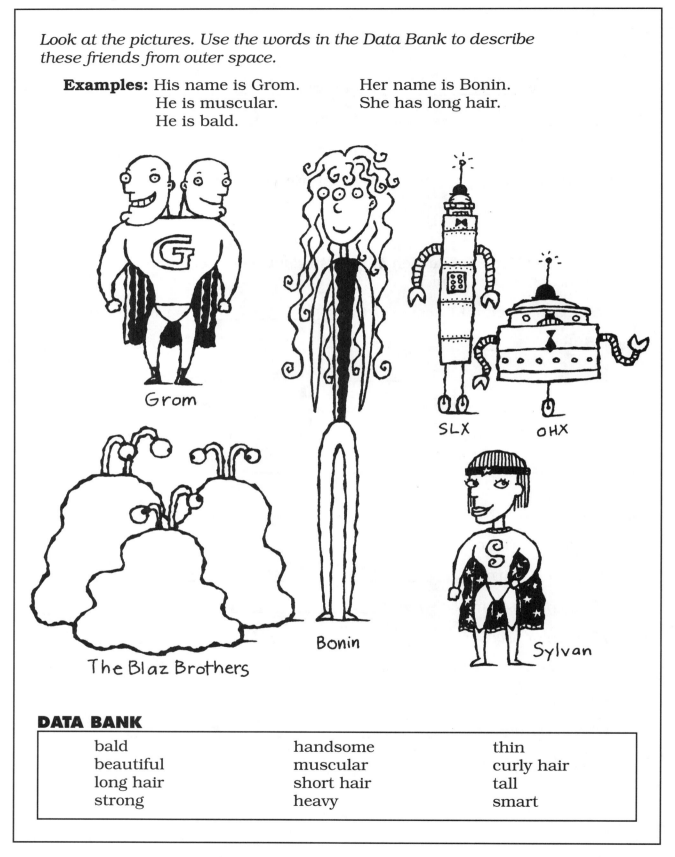

Grom

The Blaz Brothers

Bonin

SLX　　OHX

Sylvan

DATA BANK

bald	handsome	thin
beautiful	muscular	curly hair
long hair	short hair	tall
strong	heavy	smart

(Supports Student Book 2, pages 4–6) **Vocabulary development; using adjectives.** Students can work independently or with partners. Have them write their descriptions and share them with the class.

Write your own poem.

> Everybody says
>
> I look just like _____.
>
> Everybody says
>
> I'm the image of _____.
>
> Everybody says
>
> My _____ is like my _____.
>
> But I want to look like ME!

Draw a picture of yourself.

(Supports Student Book 2, page 7) **Home-School connection; cloze poetry.** Encourage free choice of words for the completion of the poem and praise all efforts. Volunteers can read their poems aloud. Have students take this page home to share with their families.

Fill out the information to create a school identification card.

School Name _____

Last Name _____ First Name _____

Age _____ Address _____

Student # _____ Locker #_____

Homeroom #_____ Homeroom Teacher _____

*Practice the dialogue below. Replace the **boldface** words with words from the Data Bank. Then fill in your schedule.*

What do you have **first** period on **Tuesday**?
I have **English**.

	1st period	2nd period	3rd period	4th period	5th period	6th period
Monday						
Tuesday						
Wednesday						
Thursday						
Friday						

DATA BANK

first = 1st	fourth = 4th	math	gym
second = 2nd	fifth = 5th	English	lunch
third = 3rd	sixth = 6th	science	social studies
		ESL	art
		health	music

(Supports Student Book 2, pages 8–9) **Vocabulary development; practicing conversations.** Review the numbers in the list with students. Have students work in pairs. Students use completed schedules for more paired conversations to practice.

Rules of Davidson School

A. *Look at the pictures. Talk about the rules.*

1. Throw trash in waste baskets.	
2. Use bulletin boards to display work.	
3. Recycle paper, bottles, cans.	
4. Clear your table in the cafeteria.	
5. Respect other people.	

B. *Discuss the rules at your school. What are the most important school rules? What are the most important class rules? Write them on the lines below.*

School Rules	**Class Rules**
_____	_____
_____	_____
_____	_____
_____	_____

(Supports Student Book 2, pages 8–9) **Comparing written language with pictures; writing.** Discuss do's and don'ts of school rules with students. Check answers in class.

Read the article about tropical rain forests on the opposite page. Put the correct information in the charts below.

Locations of tropical rain forests

_____

_____

_____

_____

_____

_____

_____

Facts about tropical rain forests

_____

_____

_____

_____

_____

_____

_____

Types of life in rain forests

_____

_____

_____

_____

_____

_____

Effects of the destruction of rain forests

_____

_____

_____

_____

_____

_____

(Supports Student Book 2, pages 10–11) **Using a chart to record information; reading comprehension.** Students can work independently or with partners. Encourage oral presentations.

Tropical Rain Forests

Tropical rain forests are found in three main areas of the world: Asia, Africa, and Central and South America. Rain forests receive between 160 and 400 inches of rain each year. In rain forests, there is no winter. Day and night have the same number of hours and the temperature is always around 80 degrees.

In these hot regions, the sun evaporates the water from the forest, clouds form, and rain recycles the water back into the forest.

Rain forests contain plants, insects, birds, reptiles, amphibians, and mammals. Millions of people also live in the rain forests of the world.

Huge areas of rain forests are being destroyed. People are cutting down the trees for lumber. They are clearing the land for farming. As trees are removed, soil falls into the rivers. This causes flooding and mud slides. The people, plants, and animals who live in the rain forest are endangered. Animals and plants lose their homes. People must learn a new way of life.

(Supports Student Book 2, pages 10–11) **Reading for a purpose; process writing.** Ask students to write a summary of the information in the reading on another piece of paper. Encourage them to use their graphic organizers on the previous page to get the facts they need. Follow process writing steps. You may want to save this assignment in students' **Assessment Portfolios.**

EL COQUI

The coquí is a tiny tree frog. It lives in the rain forests of Puerto Rico. Every night, around sunset, the coquíes sing a song.

El Coquí
A Song from Puerto Rico

El Coquí sings a sweet song at twilight.
He is singing as sleep comes to me.
When I walk all alone in the moonlight,
El Coquí sings good night from the tree.

Coquí, Coquí, Coquí, quí, quí, quí, quí,
Coquí, Coquí, Coquí, quí, quí, quí.

Draw the coquíes in the rain forest. Write sentences about your drawing.

(Supports Student Book 2, pages 12–15) **Reading for a purpose; learning language through song.** This song is on the audio tape for Theme 1. Have students listen to the song, then sing along as you play the tape again. Volunteers can share their drawings and sentences.

A. *Reread the story on pages 12–15 in your student book.*

B. *Complete the chart.*

Countries Near Puerto Rico	Languages People Speak in Puerto Rico
Festivals in Puerto Rico	**Geography and Weather in Puerto Rico**

C. *Read the sentences. Put T for true or F for false.*

____ There are many beaches in Puerto Rico.

____ Puerto Rico is too cold for swimming.

____ San Juan is the biggest city in Puerto Rico.

____ Most Puerto Ricans live on farms.

____ Most people speak Spanish in Puerto Rico.

____ A festival is a big party in the streets.

____ Puerto Ricans love their island.

(Supports Student Book 2, pages 12–15) **Reading comprehension; using a chart to record information; process writing.** Ask students to write a short essay about Puerto Rico using their graphic organizers. Follow the steps for process writing. You may want to save students' final compositions in their **Assessment Portfolios**.

Draw a picture of a beautiful place or cut out pictures from a magazine.

Here are some important geography words. Be sure you know what they mean. Are any of these in your picture? Put a check mark next to them.

DATA BANK

____ mountain	____ tree	____ delta
____ sun	____ cloud	____ ocean
____ river	____ desert	____ lake
____ moon	____ valley	____ beach

QUICK WRITE

Write about your beautiful place.

_____

_____

_____

_____

_____

_____

_____

_____

(Supports Student Book 2, pages 12–15) **Vocabulary development; process writing; computer connection.** Students draw or write a first draft of their ideas. Teacher or peer group provides feedback. Students then transfer their drawings or writing to another piece of paper. If you have access to a computer, students may complete their drawings or writing in a draw/paint program or a word processing program.

A. A secret code uses numbers or symbols to send messages. Using numbers instead of letters is the easiest code.

a	b	c	d	e	f	g	h	i	j	k	l	m
1	2	3	4	5	6	7	8	9	10	11	12	13

n	o	p	q	r	s	t	u	v	w	x	y	z
14	15	16	17	18	19	20	21	22	23	24	25	26

What is this message?

13-5-5-20   13-5   1-6-20-5-18   19-3-8-15-15-12!

To make the code harder, you can do it backwards:

a	b	c	d
26	25	24	23

Or you can start with a "key number," like 9, and add:

a	b	c	d
9	10	11	12

B. Work with a partner. Crack these codes!

20-8-9-19   3-12-1-19-19   9-19   13-25
6-1-22-15-18-9-20-5   3-12-1-19-19.

19-1-22-5   20-8-5   18-1-9-14   6-15-18-5-19-20-19.

13-25   3-15-21-14-20-18-25   9-19   22-5-18-25
2-5-1-21-20-9-6-21-12.

C. Make a new secret code. Exchange messages with your friends.

© Addison-Wesley Publishing Company

(Supports Student Book 2, pages 12–15) **Solving a puzzle; spelling.** Students work with partners. Allow time for students to share their work with the class.

15

PROCESS WRITING

The Edison Reporter

Edison Students Save Paper

The students at the Edison School are proud of their Save Paper Program. The program began when students and teachers noticed how much paper students were wasting in class. Some kids were throwing paper away when they made mistakes. They said they needed to start over.

Ms. Reeves, who teaches process writing, explained to students that mistakes and cross-outs are necessary when writing. "They are part of the process," she told the students. "Process writing starts with a first draft. A paper with changes shows your hard work. Your final paper is a corrected copy of your first draft."

Once the students realized how much paper they were wasting, they began to change their habits. John Ortiz, a student in Ms. Reeves' class, says, "Not wasting paper has helped me to understand process writing."

Students now throw their waste paper in a barrel marked "Paper" which is sent to the recycling center.

●●

Fill in the name of your school below. Use the lines to write a first draft of an article for your school newspaper. Write about a special program in your school or one you'd like to start.

The _____ Reporter

_____

_____

_____

_____

_____

_____

_____

(Supports Student Book 2, pages 16–19) **Process writing; computer connection.** Students read the sample article, then write their own. If you have access to a computer and desktop publishing software, create a classroom/school newspaper. Students can contribute to the newspaper on a regular basis.

PROCESS WRITING

(Supports Student Book 2, pages 16–19) **Process writing.** Have students follow the steps for process writing: Prewriting/Gathering Information, First Draft, Editing/Revising, Final Draft. They should use this page for their first drafts. Make sure students answer the five "W's" in their articles. You may want to save this page in students' **Assessment Portfolios.**

Read the letter from Shy Sam on page 19 of your student book. What advice can you give him? Write a letter to Shy Sam below.

Mail Box

_____

_____

_____

_____

_____

_____

_____

_____

_____

_____

_____

_____

(Supports Student Book 2, pages 16–19) **Expressing opinions; letter writing; process writing.** Reread the Mailbox letter on page 18 of the student book with students. Discuss the topic. Ask students to give their advice in a reply letter. Follow the steps for process writing. You may want to save this page in students' **Assessment Portfolios.**

CD ROM Science: Sound

YOUR TURN   Try this with your friends. Take notes.

(Supports Student Book 2, pages 16–19) **Science process skills; note-taking; writing.** Consider videotaping the experiment to share with other classes or with parents. Use as a Language Experience Activity. Have students write about the activity either individually or as a class writing experience.

SKILLS CHECK

VOCABULARY REVIEW

Circle the word in each group that does not belong. Tell why.

	A	B	C	D
1	math	science	book	geography
2	Mexico	United States	New York	Canada
3	short	fat	tall	happy
4	first	two	third	ninth
5	tree	flower	plant	building
6	moon	frog	dog	mouse
7	ocean	forest	river	lake
8	red	black	green	twelve
9	French	Spanish	Chinese	history
10	Puerto Rico	Florida	Hawaii	Bermuda

QUICK WRITE

Write about yourself. These questions will help you.

What is the name of the town or city where you live?
What is the name of your street?
Do you live in a house or an apartment building?
What do you like to do?
What don't you like to do?

_____

_____

_____

_____

_____

_____

_____

© Addison-Wesley Publishing Company

(Supports Student Book 2, page 20) **Assessment; reinforcing key vocabulary.** Work with students individually. Have students explain why they chose each word from the list. The explanation shows that the student has mastered the vocabulary. You may want to save this page in students' **Assessment Portfolios.**

HOW ARE YOU DOING?

Now I Can	yes	no	not sure
1. spell my name in English.			
2. say and write my address.			
3. say and write my phone number.			
4. say where I'm from.			
5. talk about what I look like.			
6. fill out a form.			
7. ask and talk about other people.			

Now I Know	In My Language	yes	no	not sure
mall				
favorite				
library				
college				
address				
locker				
rain forest				
gravel				
pebbles				
island				
mountain				
beach				
city				
country				
village				
town				
festival				
reserve				
lighthouse				
endangered				

___ Teacher Check

(Supports Student Book 2, page 21) **Self-assessment; Home-School connection.** Students work independently. Review the page with each student and check off your approval. Students can take a copy of this page home to share with family members. You may want to save this page in students' **Assessment Portfolios.**

1. On the tape, you heard "hello" in two different languages. Work with your class and teacher. Can you write other ways to say "hello?" Have fun singing them.

In Japanese, _____ means "hello."

In Vietnamese, _____ means "hello."

In Chinese, _____ means "hello."

In _____, _____ means "hello."

2. You can sing "good-bye" instead of "hello." You can sing "good-bye" in other languages, too. The first one is done for you. Sing all the new lines, and make up actions for saying "hello" and "good-bye."

In French, _au revoir_ means "good-bye."

In Spanish, _____ means "good-bye."

In Japanese, _____ means "good-bye."

In Vietnamese, _____ means "good-bye."

In _____, _____ means "good-bye."

3. Where do your classmates come from? Write the countries on the suitcase. Find them on a map or a globe.

22

(Supports Student Book 2, page 22) **Creating an original song verse; appreciating multicultural diversity.** Students work in a large group. Students who speak the languages represented here can fill in the blanks of the new verses. It may be necessary to provide the answers for your students.

Look at the pictures. Tell what you see. Write about the pictures.

Words I Already Know	**New Words I Have Learned**

(Supports Student Book 2, page 23) **Activating prior knowledge; self-assessment.** Students write the words they know before the lesson begins, then the words they have learned at the end of the lesson. You may want to save this page in students' **Assessment Portfolios**.

Reread the story that begins on page 24 of your student book.
Fill in the blanks below.

In my mother's _____

All _____

I _____ and work;

_____ night

I _____ .

The walls _____ close around me

In a _____ way.

_____ can see them;

I _____ feel them;

I live with _____ .

This house is _____ to me,

It _____ me;

I like it,

My _____ house.

In my mother's _____

There _____ a fireplace

The fireplace _____ the fire

On _____ nights the fire is bright

On cold nights the fire is _____

The fire is _____ there

To _____ me see

To keep me _____ .

© Addison-Wesley Publishing Company

(Supports Student Book 2, pages 24–27) **Cloze exercise.** Before students begin this page, reread aloud, or play the tape of, the student book pages. Then have students work independently.

Find the words in the story that mean the same as the following ideas. Write them in the chart.

The girl likes the walls in her mother's house.	
The fire in the house is important.	
People do lots of things in the plaza.	
There are many houses in the village.	

(Supports Student Book 2, pages 24–27) **Reading comprehension; using a chart.** Students complete the page independently. Check answers in class.

25

Write T for True or F for False beside the sentences below.

1. _____ The girl likes the walls in her mother's house.

2. _____ The girl sleeps all day in her mother's house.

3. _____ The house is good to the girl.

4. _____ There are three fireplaces in the mother's house.

5. _____ The girl likes the fireplace.

6. _____ The people sing and dance in the plaza.

7. _____ The people sleep in the plaza.

8. _____ The houses are close together.

9. _____ The plaza is only for girls and women.

10. _____ The girl does not like the plaza.

QUICK WRITE
Write about your own house.

_____

_____

_____

_____

_____

_____

_____

_____

_____

_____

_____

(Supports Student Book 2, pages 24–27) **Reading comprehension; distinguishing true-false statements; writing.** Students work independently. Ask students to change false statements to true statements. Encourage oral presentations. You may want to save this page in students' **Assessment Portfolios.**

Look at the pictures. Read about these buildings.

There are many different kinds of buildings. Skyscrapers are very tall. Skyscrapers are in cities. People work and live in skyscrapers. People live in apartment houses and in condominiums. Some people live in two-family or three-family houses. Some people live in single family houses. Lots of people live in trailers and mobile homes, too.

Some people build tree houses. Other people build small houses for their dogs or very small houses for wild birds. Look around your neighborhood. Describe the buildings you see.

_____

_____

_____

_____

_____

_____

_____

_____

(Supports Student Book 2, pages 24–27) **Reading for a purpose; writing.** Students complete the page independently. Encourage oral presentations. You may want to save this page in students' **Assessment Portfolios.**

Look at the pictures. Then write the answers to the questions. Use in, on, under, beside or between. There is more than one way to answer each question. Compare your answers with a partner's answers. Are they the same or different?

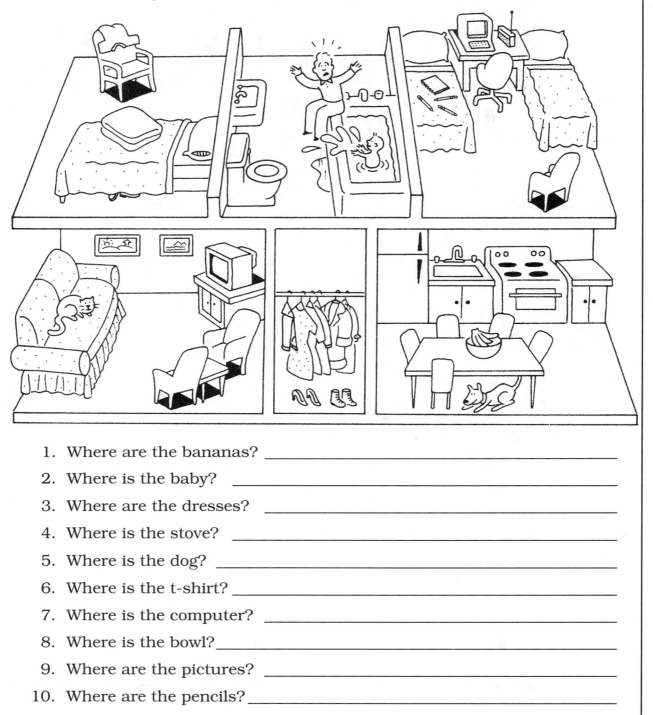

1. Where are the bananas? _____

2. Where is the baby? _____

3. Where are the dresses? _____

4. Where is the stove? _____

5. Where is the dog? _____

6. Where is the t-shirt? _____

7. Where is the computer? _____

8. Where is the bowl? _____

9. Where are the pictures? _____

10. Where are the pencils? _____

(Supports Student Book 2, pages 28–29) **Describing locations with prepositons; comparing/contrasting.**
Students work independently first, then compare answers with a partner. Check answers in class.

Planning a Party

Mr. and Mrs. Davis are planning a party for their son, Steve. He's going to be sixteen years old next month.

"How many people should we invite, Sam?" asked Mrs. Davis.

"Let's see, Evelyn. There are fourteen family members and ten of Steve's friends.

"Twenty-four people! How much food will we need?"

"Steve's friends eat a lot. We need to buy lots of food."

"Let's make a list."

Look at the lists. Answer the questions.

Shopping List	Guest List
3 gallons of ice cream 1 large cake 10 gallons of lemonade 15 pounds of chicken 1 bag of rice 6 loaves of bread	Grandma & Grandpa Hernandez Grandma & Grandpa Davis Uncle Fred & Aunt Jennifer Tom, Jill, Susan (cousins) Uncle Guillermo, Aunt Isabel Tony, Peter, Michael (cousins) Keisha, Larry, Tyrone, Efrain, Duc, May, Nelson, Jack, Kelly, Diana (Steve's friends)

1. How many grandparents are they going to invite? _____

2. How many cousins are they going to invite? _____

3. How much ice cream are they going to buy? _____

4. How much chicken are they going to buy?_____

5. How many family members are they going to invite? _____

6. How much lemonade are they going to serve? _____

7. How many friends are they going to invite? _____

8. How much rice are they going to buy?_____

(Supports Student Book 2, pages 28–29) **Reading for a purpose; describing quantity.** Students complete the page independently. Check answers in class.

Make Healthy Meals

Look at the Food Pyramid on page 30 in your student book. Use the food pyramid to plan healthy meals in the boxes below. Write the foods in the boxes. You may also draw pictures of the foods.

Breakfast	Lunch
Dinner	**Snack**

Now count the servings of each kind of food.

How many fruits do you have? ____

How many vegetables do you have? ____

How many grains do you have? ____

How many dairy products do you have? ____

How many fats do you have? ____

© Addison-Wesley Publishing Company

(Supports Student Book 2, pages 30–31) **Food vocabulary; using a chart to record information; describing quantity; process writing.** After students complete the page, have them write a composition about healthy eating. Follow process writing steps. You may want to save students' writing in their **Assessment Portfolios.**

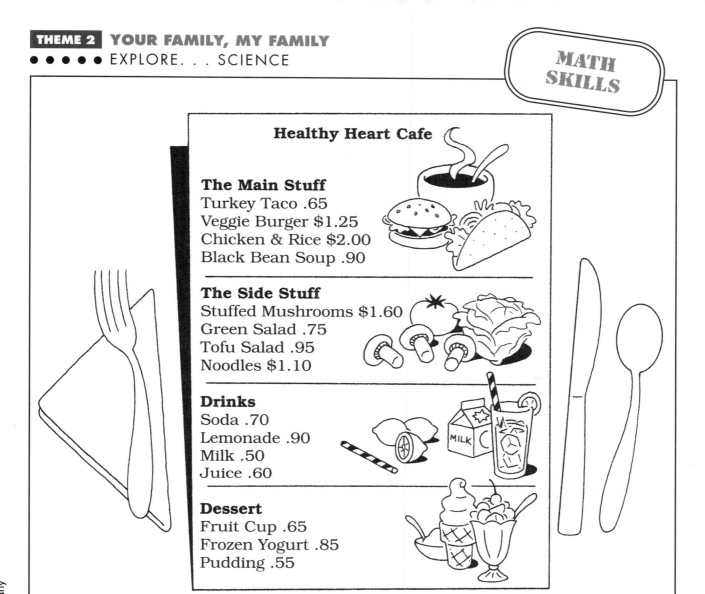

Healthy Heart Cafe

The Main Stuff
Turkey Taco .65
Veggie Burger $1.25
Chicken & Rice $2.00
Black Bean Soup .90

The Side Stuff
Stuffed Mushrooms $1.60
Green Salad .75
Tofu Salad .95
Noodles $1.10

Drinks
Soda .70
Lemonade .90
Milk .50
Juice .60

Dessert
Fruit Cup .65
Frozen Yogurt .85
Pudding .55

1. Show the menu to two friends. Ask them to choose a meal. Write their meals below.

_____   _____

_____   _____

_____   _____

_____   _____

Total _____   **Total** _____

2. Add the cost of their meals. Write the total amounts above.
3. You have $2.80. What will you choose from the menu?

(Supports Student Book, pages 30–31) **Math content skills; data collection; interviewing.** Students complete the page independently. Encourage oral presentations.

31

READING SKILLS

The Inside Family

Meet the Moore family. They live in Alaska where the weather is cold most of the time. During the long winter, they like to stay inside by the fire. Stephan, the oldest son loves to cook and makes the family wonderful meals.

Dad and Mom both love to read and the whole family likes to watch sports on TV. The children like to play board games together. They talk to their friends on the phone. Some of their friends like to go skiing, skating, or sledding. The Moores enjoy hearing about their friends' adventures, but they don't like to do things outdoors when it's cold. They are happy to be inside their cozy house.

A. *Answer the following questions about the Moore family.*

1. Where do the Moores live?

   _____

2. What do Mom and Dad like to do?

   _____

3. What does the family like to do together?

   _____

4. What does Stephan like to do?

   _____

5. What do the Moores not like to do?

   _____

6. What makes the Moores happy?

   _____

B. *Is your family like the Moore family? Why or why not? Write about it.*

   _____

   _____

   _____

   _____

(Supports Student Book, pages 32–34) **Reading for a purpose; writing.** Before students complete the page, discuss different meanings of the word "like" such as "What do they like to do?" versus "What are they like?" Check answers in class.

READING SKILLS

The Outside Family

Meet the Yamamoto family. They are an outside family. They are active, athletic people. They live on the island of Oahu in Hawaii and they love the warm weather. They like to go bike riding in the afternoon. The kids, Patty and Chris, like to play frisbee with their father after dinner.

Mrs. Yamamoto has a beautiful garden. She likes to spend a lot of time in it. It is one of the most beautiful gardens on the island.

The Yamamotos are planning a summer vacation of outside fun. They are going to camp at Volcano National Park on the Big Island of Hawaii. They are going to hike, play volleyball, and swim. Mr. Yamamoto plans to cook outside every night. "I love to cook and eat outdoors," says Mr. Yamamoto."

A. *Answer the questions about the Yamamoto family.*

1. What do the Yamamotos like to do?

   _____

2. What do the kids like to do in the afternoon?

   _____

3. What does Mrs. Yamamoto like to do?

   _____

4. Where is the Yamamoto family going to spend their vacation?

   _____

5. What are the Yamamotos going to do on their vacation?

   _____

6. Why does Mr. Yamamoto want to cook outdoors every night?

   _____

B. *Is your family like the Yamamoto family? Why or why not? Write about it.*

   _____

   _____

   _____

(Supports Student Book 2, pages 32–34) **Reading for a purpose; writing.** Students complete the page independently. Check answers in class.

33

MATH SKILLS

Lin Quong owns the Party Planner store. She has chosen some party favors to sell in her store. She has filled out the order form. Use the order form to answer the questions.

Balloons (pkg)	7	$1.29
Top Hats	3	5.23
Party Hats	8	2.31
Candles (pkg)	5	.75
Horns	9	4.19
Masks	6	4.19

1. How much do six masks cost? _____

2. How much do five packages of candles cost? _____

3. What is the cost of one horn? _____

4. How much more does a top hat cost than a party hat? _____

5. How much are seven packages of balloons? _____

6. What is the total cost of the order? _____

(Supports Student Book 2, pages 32–34) **Math content skills.** Students may work individually or with partners. Check answers in class.

Make Your Own Kite

You will need:
- a paper bag
- markers
- a ruler
- two 16" long sticks, about the thickness of a pencil
- tape
- a pencil
- scissors
- a roll of string

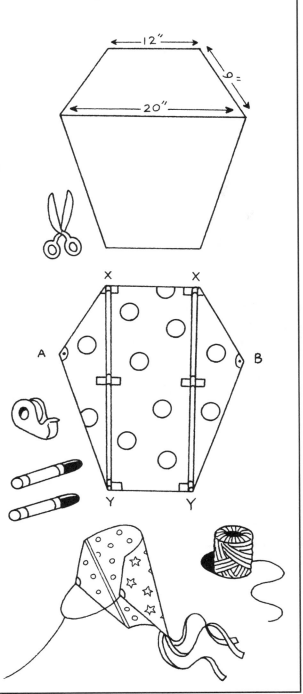

1. Cut open the paper bag. Lay it flat on a table or on the floor.

2. Use a marker. Draw the kite pattern on the bag. Use a ruler. Make sure your kite has the same measurements as shown here.

3. Cut out the pattern. Decorate both sides with markers.

4. Lay the sticks from X to Y, as shown. Attach the sticks to the kite with tape.

5. Use a pencil. Punch one hole at A. Punch another hole at B.

6. Cut a piece of string 40" long. Tie one end of the string at A. Tie one end of the string at B.

7. At the very center of the string, tie a small loop.

8. Tie the end of your roll of string to the loop. Hold the roll of string in your hand. Find a wind and run!

(Supports Student Book 2, page 35) **Reading and following directions; measuring.** When activity is complete, discuss as a class. Ask students to take notes and then write about the experience. Follow the steps for process writing.

PROCESS WRITING

The Edison Reporter

An Evening of Fashion

Last Sunday, the eighth grade held a fashion show to raise money for a gift to the school. It is a tradition at Edison school for the graduating class to present a gift to the school. It is a way of saying "thank you and don't forget us" to the teachers and other staff as well as to the younger students.

Marr's department store provided the clothes for the fashion show. Students modeled spring and summer outfits for teenagers of all sizes and tastes. Parents modeled clothes for adults. Patrick Badakian, class president, said, "We wanted to attract a lot of people, so we included clothes that our parents would like."

The favorite clothes of the evening were the prom and party clothes for both boys and girls. Marr's also provided two $100 gift certificates as door prizes. They were won by Mr. Aldo Fonseca and Ms. Dorothy Cabot.

The fashion show was a great success. According to Patrick Badakian, the eighth grade raised enough money to buy a beautiful brick planter for the lobby of the school. Patrick is also happy to report that there is enough money left over for a pizza party on the graduates' last day of class.

● ●

Fill in the name of your school below. Use the lines to write a first draft of an article for your school newspaper. Write about a recent event in your school or community.

The _____ Reporter

_____

_____

_____

_____

_____

_____

_____

(Supports Student Book 2, pages 36–39) **Process writing; computer connection.** Students read the sample article, then write their own. If you have access to a computer and desktop publishing software, create a classroom/school newspaper. Students can contribute to the newspaper on a regular basis.

_____

_____

_____

_____

_____

_____

_____

_____

_____

_____

_____

_____

_____

_____

_____

_____

_____

_____

_____

_____

_____

_____

_____

_____

_____

_____

(Supports Student Book 2, pages 36–39) **Process writing.** Have students follow the steps for process writing: Prewriting/Gathering Information, First Draft, Editing/Revising, Final Draft. They should use this page for their first drafts. Make sure students answer the five "W's" in their articles. You may want to save this page in students' **Assessment Portfolios.**

PROCESS WRITING

Read the letter from Feeling the Blues on page 39 of your student book. Can you help with the problem? Write a letter to Feeling the Blues.

Mail Box

_____

_____

_____

_____

_____

_____

_____

_____

_____

_____

_____

_____

(Supports Student Book 2, pages 36–39) **Expressing opinions; letter writing; process writing.** Reread the Mailbox letter on page 38 of the student book with students. Discuss the topic. Ask students to give their advice in a reply letter. Follow the steps for process writing. You may want to save this page in students' **Assessment Portfolios.**

CD ROM Science: Vacuums

YOUR TURN   Draw conclusions. Why does the egg fall into the bottle?

(Supports Student Book 2, pages 36–39) **Science process skills.** Use as a Language Experience Activity. Have students write about the activity either individually or as a class writing experience. You may want to include this writing in students' **Assessment Portfolios.**

SKILLS CHECK

VOCABULARY REVIEW
Circle the word in each group that does not belong. Tell why.

	A	B	C	D
1	refrigerator	kitchen	bathroom	bedroom
2	sink	coat	refrigerator	stove
3	broccoli	spinach	carrots	cake
4	breakfast	rice	lunch	dinner
5	library	read	play	shop
6	beside	between	under	corn
7	ring	bracelet	necklace	igloo
8	computer	chair	sofa	bench
9	house	skyscraper	apartment	kitchen
10	city	village	state	sky

QUICK WRITE
Write about your favorite foods.

There are many foods I like.

_____

_____

_____

_____

_____

_____

_____

_____

_____

40

(Supports Student Book 2, page 40) **Assessment; reinforcing key vocabulary.** Work with students individually. Have students explain why they chose each word from the list. The explanation shows that the student has mastered the vocabulary. You may want to save this page in students **Assessment Portfolios.**

HOW ARE YOU DOING?

Now I Can	yes	no	not sure
1. name the rooms in a house.			
2. name furniture and appliances.			
3. name kinds of buildings.			
4. use prepositions.			
5. name some healthy foods.			
6. plan healthy meals.			
7. build a kite.			

Now I Know	In My Language	yes	no	not sure
fireplace				
plaza				
recommended				
healthy				
calcium				
vitamin				
daily				
salsa				
inside				
outside				
hummingbird				
fruits				
vegetables				
dairy				
meat				
protein				
grains				
meals				
gallons				
pounds				

___ Teacher Check

(Supports Student Book 2, page 41) **Self-assessment; Home-School connection.** Students work independently. Review the page with each student and check off your approval. Students can take a copy of this page home to share with family members. You may want to save this page in students' **Assessment Portfolios.**

Make a Birthday Card

You will need:
- a piece of paper
- markers or crayons
- scraps of colored paper
- scissors
- glue

1. Fold a piece of paper in half.

2. On the front of the card, write the words HAPPY BIRTHDAY in large letters. Decorate the letters with colored markers or crayons. You can also draw a picture on the front of the card.

3. Cut out small shapes from colored paper. Glue them onto the card to look like confetti.

4. Open the card and write a birthday message to a friend or family member.

5. Add more confetti inside the card.

6. Don't forget to sign it!

(Supports Student Book 2, page 42) **Reading and following directions; Home-School connection.** Discuss birthday traditions before students begin this activity. Students work independently, then take their cards home to share with a family member or friend.

Look at the picture. Tell what you see. Write about the picture.

Words I Already Know	**New Words I Have Learned**

(Supports Student Book 2, page 43) **Activating prior knowledge; self-assessment.** Students write the words they know before the lesson begins, then the words they have learned at the end of the lesson. You may want to save this page in students' **Assessment Portfolios**.

READING SKILLS

Read carefully. Choose the best answer. Write the letter on the line.

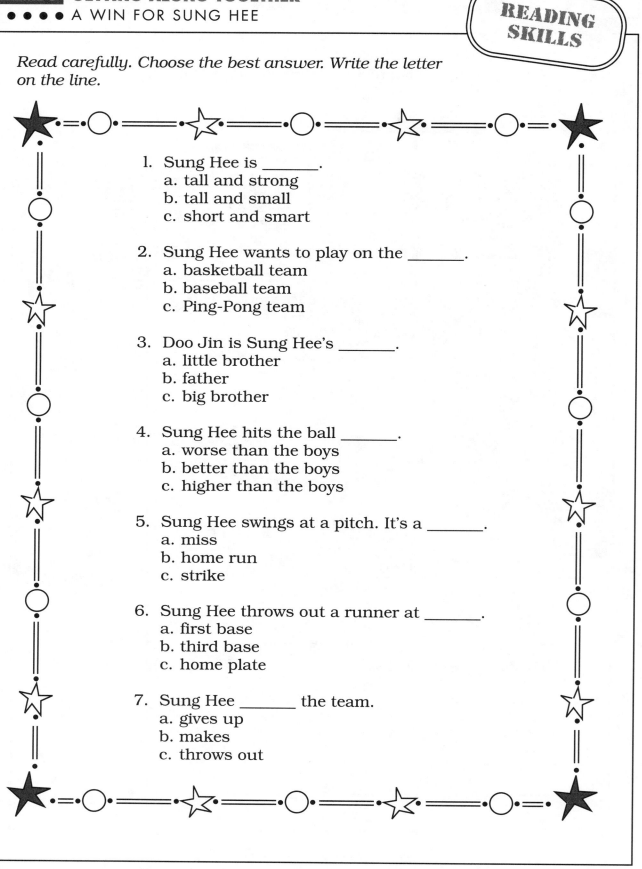

1. Sung Hee is _____.
   a. tall and strong
   b. tall and small
   c. short and smart

2. Sung Hee wants to play on the _____.
   a. basketball team
   b. baseball team
   c. Ping-Pong team

3. Doo Jin is Sung Hee's _____.
   a. little brother
   b. father
   c. big brother

4. Sung Hee hits the ball _____.
   a. worse than the boys
   b. better than the boys
   c. higher than the boys

5. Sung Hee swings at a pitch. It's a _____.
   a. miss
   b. home run
   c. strike

6. Sung Hee throws out a runner at _____.
   a. first base
   b. third base
   c. home plate

7. Sung Hee _____ the team.
   a. gives up
   b. makes
   c. throws out

© Addison-Wesley Publishing Company

(Supports Student Book 2, pages 44–46) **Reading comprehension; multiple-choice questions.** Check answers in class.

Read carefully. Put the sentences in the correct order. Write the numbers on the lines.

_____ Sung Hee hits the ball.

_____ Sung Hee wants to try out for the team.

_____ Sung Hee swings at a pitch.

_____ Sung Hee's brother watches the tryouts.

_____ A batter hits the ball on the ground.

_____ It's a home run.

_____ Sung Hee throws a runner out at home.

_____ Sung Hee feels nervous.

_____ Sung Hee makes the team.

_____ Sung Hee plays first base.

Find the words in the story that mean the same as the following ideas.

The coach only wants boys on the baseball team.	_____ _____
Sung Hee does not stay away from the tryouts.	_____ _____
Sung Hee does very well at the tryouts.	_____ _____
Roberto thinks Sung Hee is a good player.	_____ _____
The coach lets Sung Hee play on the team.	_____ _____

(Supports Student Book 2, pages 44–46) **Reading comprehension; sequencing.** Students work independently. Check answers in class.

45

READING SKILLS

Complete this summary chart about "A Win for Sung Hee."

Who are the characters in the story? _____

_____

_____

What happens at tryouts? _____

_____

_____

What happens at the end of the story? _____

_____

_____

Now tell if the following statements are True or False.

1. _____ Sung Hee is a champion Ping-Pong player.

2. _____ Sung Hee loves to hit the ball.

3. _____ The coach wants girls and boys on the team.

4. _____ Sung Hee goes to the tryouts.

5. _____ Doo Jin and Roberto are at the tryouts.

6. _____ Sung Hee can't hit the ball at the tryouts.

7. _____ Sung Hee hits a home run at the tryouts.

8. _____ Sung Hee plays first base.

9. _____ Roberto thinks Sung Hee is a bad player.

10. _____ Sung Hee is on the baseball team at the end of the story.

(Supports Student Book 2, pages 46–48) **Reading comprehension; summarizing; distinguishing true-false statements.** Students work independently. Ask them to rewrite false statements as true statements. Encourage oral presentations.

Read the poem on page 47 of your student book again. Write a poem about your favorite sport. Think of things you see, hear, smell, taste, and do at this sporting event. Illustrate your poem.

I love _____

I smell _____.

I taste _____;

I see _____;

I hear _____.

The fans _____;

The players _____.

Let the game begin!

(Supports Student Book 2, page 47) **Creative writing.** Final copies of students' poems can be collected and put in a class book, displayed on a bulletin board, or added to students' **Assessment Portfolios**.

DATA COLLECTION

Complete the activity chart by checking (√) the column(s) that are true for you.

Activity	I can	I can't	I like to	I don't like to	I want to learn how to
cook					
dance					
do math					
fly a plane					
skate					
play baseball					
play basketball					
play soccer					
ride a bike					
sew					
sing					
write a poem					
knit					
drive a car					
swim					
use a computer					

Compare your answers with a partner's answers. Fill in the Venn Diagram with your information.

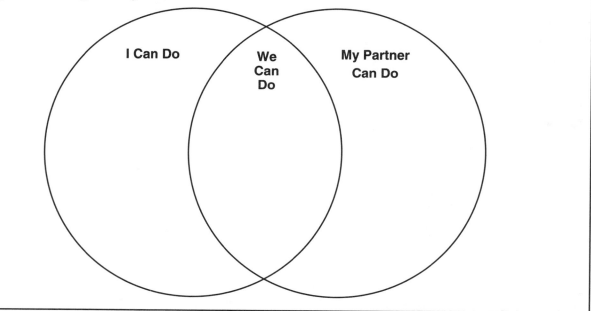

I Can Do   We Can Do   My Partner Can Do

(Supports Student Book 2, pages 48–49) **Data collection; providing information about self; comparing/contrasting; using a chart to record information.** Ask students to write a composition based on the information in their graphic organizers. Follow the steps for process writing. You may want to save this page and students' writing in their **Assessment Portfolios.**

Keisha's Day

Talk about the pictures. Answer the questions.

1. What does Keisha do at 6:00?
2. What does she do at 6:45?
3. What does she do at 6:55?
4. What does she do at 11:00?
5. When does she practice baseball?
6. When does she pick up her brother at daycare?
7. When does she help prepare dinner?
8. When does she wash dishes?
9. When does she go to sleep?

(Supports Student Book 2, pages 48–49) **Telling time; discussing daily schedules.** Students discuss the page as a class, then answer the questions with partners. Check answers in class.

At the Game

You need to buy 26 tickets for a sports event. You have $348 and must spend it all. What type of tickets can you buy? How many of each type can you buy?

Suppose you had $348 to buy 26 tickets. This time you can spend all the money on tickets or save part of it to use for another activity. What combination(s) of back and front seats can you buy that would cost less then $348? How can you save the most money?

BASEBALL GAME
FRONT SEATS $18
BACK SEATS $12

$18

$12

© Addison-Wesley Publishing Company

(Supports Student Book 2, pages 50–51) **Reading for a purpose; math content skills; solving problems logically.** Students may complete the page individually or with partners. Help students with strategies for solving math-word problems.

Read the notices on the bulletin board. Answer the questions.

1. Where is the Computer Club meeting?
2. Where is baseball practice?
3. Where is the Science Club meeting?
4. When is cheerleading practice?
5. When is the Junior Honor Society meeting?
6. When is band practice?

Practice the following dialogue with a partner. Change the
boldface words *for other words from the bulletin board.*
Take turns.

What are we doing at **band practice** today?
We're having a guest speaker.
That sounds interesting. Where's the meeting?
It's **in the Band Room**.

(Supports Student Book 2, pages 50-51) **Reading for a purpose; practicing conversations.** Check answers
in class. Have students practice more paired conversations.

51

School Mascots

Many schools have a school mascot. It is an animal or symbol that stands for the school. The school mascot is usually the mascot for all the school sports teams. Look at the mascots below. How many can you name? Work with a partner. Use the Data Bank at the bottom of the page to help you.

Draw a picture of your school mascot. (If you don't have a school mascot, draw one you like.)

DATA BANK

bear	viking	ram
fox	bulldog	comet
owl	leopard	eagle
tornado	pirate	mustang
bull	wolf	tiger
knight	cowboy	dolphin
panther	lion	

(Supports Student Book 2, pages 52–55) **Vocabulary development.** Check answers in class.

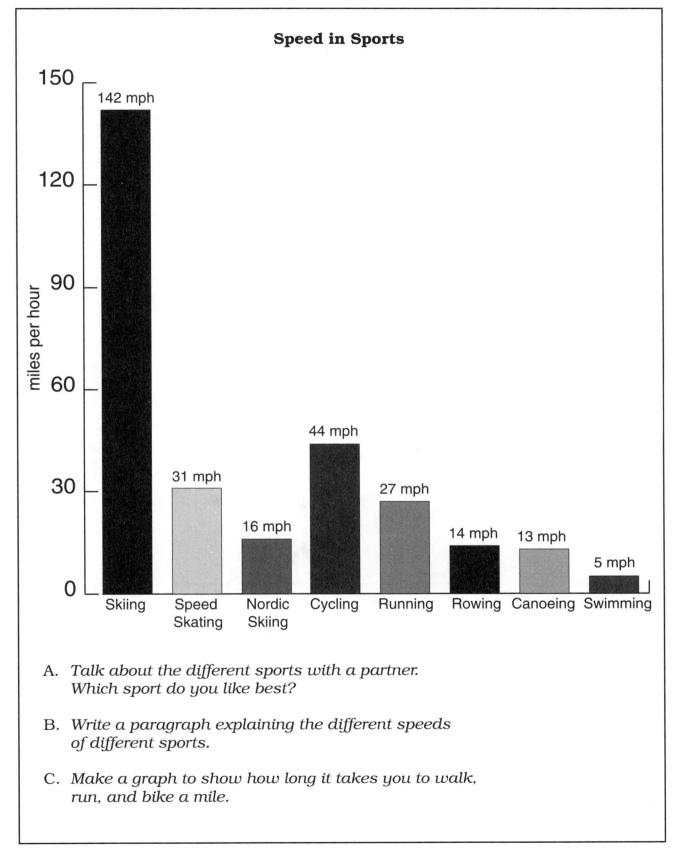

Speed in Sports

A. *Talk about the different sports with a partner.*
   Which sport do you like best?

B. *Write a paragraph explaining the different speeds*
   of different sports.

C. *Make a graph to show how long it takes you to walk,*
   run, and bike a mile.

(Supports Student Book 2, pages 52–55) **Reading a bar graph; writing; graphing.** Explain that mph stands
for miles per hour. Students discuss graph with partners, then complete exercises B and C independently.
Encourage oral presentations.

53

Safety First

A. *It's fun and exciting to go fast, but going fast can be dangerous in sports. Read and learn the following safety rules.*

In the Water
- You should always wear a life jacket when you are in a boat.
- You should never swim alone.
- You should never dive in shallow water.

Exercise and Weather
- You should drink plenty of fluids when you exercise outside on hot days.
- You should wear several layers of clothing when you are exercising outside on cold days.
- You should check the weather and listen to warnings about dangerous conditions.

Equipment
- You should always wear a helmet when you ride a bike.
- You should always wear a helmet and elbow, knee, and wrist pads when in-line skating.
- You should always ride your bike in the same direction as the traffic.
- You should always wear a seat belt when riding in a car.

B. *What exercise is an important part of your life? What safety rules do you follow? Write about it.*

_____

_____

_____

_____

_____

_____

_____

_____

Sports Word Search

```
J A M U N I F O R M C N G O O P L J G I B K N P N H E F B C A K
E K C K F O L F H G U F O U L Q L P L K H B E L P I R T B D J I
L F I I L L A C N R E R J L L Q N K Q O H F G A I I B H K A H C
B E B N M C O A E D A E M O G D H O A C C L H K F A N S L B G K
I P D P J J G M I P G F P A L A Q E H C L Q G K C G C H J N J G
G M D K L J O P L P E E L B N N A K Q I H H A O N M I J G M F P
O N L G K H K M C P I R E F M I F O C J Q H J B K B E O I D F E
H G B L Q Q C N B J Q E I C I K N B N L B J O A M L G I M J H M
E B E D A P P L D J H E D O O D N K P O A K A G J I C Q A F N C
E G L Q J B I J M Q D E N G D A K J N B D A P I K L O M G B Q L
Q G G E L L E L E J A U F O Q G C P J G O F G I F J M F I E Q M
A I N A A O B S L N P E M N F S P H D A R L A F C L P H N G A G
P O I L E O H F A A C I I P F D T O O E I E L K K D H O B G Q B
C B S M M I Q G P B B D D I I O M R G N L D C A D L J C L S E C
B G P R A C T I C E J T B C E R Q E I G Q L L C B L A K J T K H
H D Q D A E K I D K E O E E P P E I E K K Q H J O T I E P A M N
I C A E J J T N A G G G T K F J D L J K E S A D B S O Y N D D Q
H E A O C H P N J J P A P F S D Q A G N L H W N L G O O C I E O
B N J I B L A I Q G L G N Q B A D O Q A A D A I P B I M F U P E
M G L N F I H N G P H I I F E J B G H C A P W H N M I L L M P P
C E L B U O D G E T R Y O U T S K O L H A L B O J G G P M P K N
I C E L Q I O M M A S C O T A G N M P H O G D B R F C P I L H G
N M L E P A O N P F J K L E B G G B E F L E D A M C E O K M M Q
F H H G N H A E H P D L Q A E C M C I S R E D A E L R E E H C N
```

BASEBALL	GOALIE	SINGLE
BASKETBALL	HOCKEY	SOCCER
CHEERLEADERS	HOME PLATE	STADIUM
COACH	HOME RUN	STRIKE
CROWD	INNING	SWING
DOUBLE	KICK	TEAM
FANS	MASCOT	TRIPLE
FOOTBALL	PERIOD	TRYOUTS
FOUL	PRACTICE	UMPIRE
GOAL	REFEREE	UNIFORM

(Supports Student Book 2, pages 52–55) **Solving a puzzle; reinforcing key vocabulary; spelling.** Students may work independently or with partners.

PROCESS WRITING

The Edison Reporter

Mrs. Sanchez Named Teacher of the Year

Congratulations to Mrs. Sanchez of Room 7B. She was named teacher of the year for the Madison County School District. Mrs. Sanchez has been a teacher for 17 years. She has taught every grade from kindergarten to grade 8, but she says her favorite grade is grade 7.

"I love seventh grade students. They really work hard. They take all their classes very seriously. We read some wonderful novels in the seventh grade, too. Come by my class anytime and you can see how great seventh grade is."

Everyone knows Mrs. Sanchez is an excellent teacher. Edison School is lucky to have such a wonderful teacher. We can all be proud of her.

● ●

Fill in the name of your school below. Use the lines to write a first draft of an article for your school newspaper. Write about someone you admire.

The _____ Reporter

_____

_____

_____

_____

_____

_____

_____

_____

_____

_____

_____

(Supports Student Book 2, pages 56–59) **Process writing; computer connection.** Students read the sample article, then write their own. If you have access to a computer and desktop publishing software, create a classroom/school newspaper. Students can contribute to the newspaper on a regular basis.

PROCESS WRITING

(Supports Student Book 2, pages 56–59) **Process writing.** Have students follow the steps for process writing: Prewriting/Gathering Information, First Draft, Editing/Revising, Final Draft. They should use this page for their first drafts. Make sure students answer the five "W's" in their articles. You may want to save this page in students' **Assessment Portfolios.**

Read the letter from J.R. on page 59 of your student book.
Write a letter telling J.R. your ideas about how to save money.

Mail Box

_____

_____

_____

_____

_____

_____

_____

_____

_____

_____

_____

_____

_____

_____

_____

(Supports Student Book 2, pages 56–59) **Expressing opinions; letter writing; process writing.** Reread the
Mailbox letter on page 58 of the student book with students. Discuss the topic. Ask students to give their
advice in a reply letter. Follow the steps for process writing. You may want to save this page in students'
Assessment Portfolios.

SCIENCE PROCESS SKILLS

CD ROM Science: Coin Toss

	Heads	**Tails**
Toss 1		
Toss 2		
Toss 3		
Toss 4		
Toss 5		
Toss 6		
Toss 7		
Toss 8		
Toss 9		
Toss 10		

YOUR TURN Collect and record data. Work with a partner. Toss a coin ten times. Record your results. Calculate how many times you got heads and how many times you got tails. Was it the same as Byte and Meg?

Draw conclusions. Compare your results with others in the class. Did everyone get the same results?

(Supports Student Book 2, pages 56–59) **Science process skills; using a chart to record information; comparing/contrasting.** Consider videotaping the experiment to share with other classes or with parents. Use as a Language Experience Activity. Have students write about the activity either individually or as a class writing experience. You may want to include this writing in students' **Assessment Portfolios.**

ASSESSMENT

SKILLS CHECK

VOCABULARY REVIEW

Circle the word in each group that does not belong. Tell why.

	A	B	C	D
1	library	truck	hospital	supermarket
2	checkers	baseball	basketball	soccer
3	bear	bull	lion	dolphin
4	umpire	coach	doctor	pitcher
5	Korean	friendly	French	Chinese
6	gym	library	auditorium	laundromat
7	Monday	Tuesday	September	Sunday
8	January	February	December	Wednesday
9	drugstore	truck	bus	train
10	knight	pirate	cowboy	eagle

QUICK WRITE
Write about places you go after school and what you do there.

_____

_____

_____

_____

_____

_____

_____

_____

_____

_____

(Supports Student Book 2, page 60) **Assessment; reinforcing key vocabulary.** Work with students individually. Have students explain why they chose each word from the list. The explanation shows that the student
has mastered the vocabulary. You may want to save this page in students' **Assessment Portfolios.**

HOW ARE YOU DOING?

Now I Can	yes	no	not sure
1. tell what people are doing.			
2. ask and answer questions.			
3. complete a Venn diagram.			
4. write a poem.			
5. tell about my everyday activities.			
6. read a bulletin board.			
7. talk about school rules.			

Now I Know	In My Language	yes	no	not sure
tall				
strong				
baseball				
tryouts				
coach				
team				
cheer				
soccer				
goal				
score				
athlete				
players				
fans				
tickets				
practice				
meeting				
mascot				
safety				
exercise				
equipment				

___ Teacher Check

(Supports Student Book 2, page 61) **Self-assessment; Home-School connection.** Students work independently. Review the page with each student and check off your approval. Students can take a copy of this page home to share with family members. You may want to save this page in students' **Assessment Portfolios.**

A. What do you say yes or no about every day? Make a list
on the lines below. Compare your list with a partner's list.
How are they different? How are they alike?

_____

_____

_____

_____

_____

_____

B. Can you say yes or no about going to school? Who decides
if you go to school? What are some other things you can't
say yes or no about? List them below. Write who decides
these things for you.

_____

_____

_____

_____

_____

_____

C. When will you be able to make these decisions for yourself?
Talk about this with your teacher and class.

© Addison-Wesley Publishing Company

(Supports Student Book 2, page 62) **Providing information about self; writing.** Students complete the page
independently. Encourage oral presentations.

Look at the pictures. Tell what you see. Write about the pictures.

Words I Already Know	New Words I Have Learned

(Supports Student Book 2, page 63) **Activating prior knowledge; self-assessment.** Students write the words they know before the lesson begins, then the words they have learned at the end of the lesson. You may want to save this page in students' **Assessment Portfolios**.

Reread the poem on pages 64–67 of your student book. Write a dream story of your own. The words on the next page can help you. You can use any words you like, too.

I went all the way to _____
(1)

In a dream one night.

I crossed over the _____
(2)

In a _____, _____ jump
(3)   (4)

And landed in _____.
(1)

I went to the city

And shopped in the marketplace

For _____ and _____.
(5)   (6)

I rode on a _____;
(7)

I danced a _____ dance
(8)

To the drums of my uncles;

I sang a _____ song
(9)

In a circle with new-old friends.

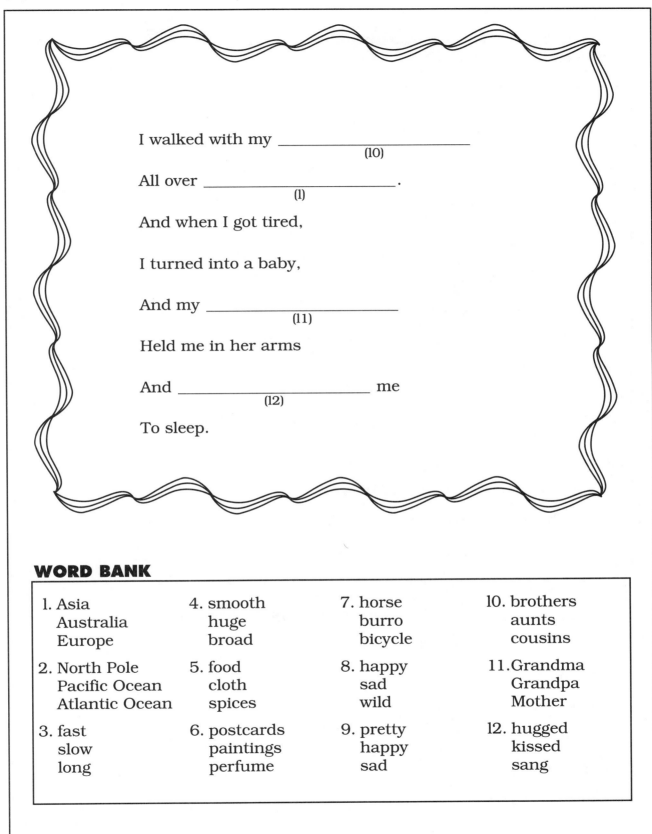

I walked with my _____
(10)

All over _____.
(1)

And when I got tired,

I turned into a baby,

And my _____
(11)

Held me in her arms

And _____ me
(12)

To sleep.

WORD BANK

1. Asia Australia Europe	4. smooth huge broad	7. horse burro bicycle	10. brothers aunts cousins
2. North Pole Pacific Ocean Atlantic Ocean	5. food cloth spices	8. happy sad wild	11. Grandma Grandpa Mother
3. fast slow long	6. postcards paintings perfume	9. pretty happy sad	12. hugged kissed sang

(Supports Student Book 2, pages 64–67) **Guided writing; cloze exercise.** Students complete the page independently. Encourage free choice of words for the completion of the poem and praise all efforts. Volunteers can read their poems aloud.

Complete the following summary chart to tell what happened in the poem "Africa Dream."

Where did the girl go? _____ _____ _____	
What did she see? _____ _____ _____	
What did she do? _____ _____ _____	

Now complete the summary of the poem.

Africa Dream

A girl dreamed she went far away. She jumped over the

_____ and landed in Africa. In _____ she went to

the city and shopped in the marketplace. She read strange words in old

_____, and she understood them. She rode a

_____ through the crowds.

She went to the _____. She danced and _____

with her family and friends. She walked with her _____ all

over Africa.

When she got _____, she turned into a baby. One of her

long-ago relatives rocked her to _____.

(Supports Student Book 2, pages 64–67) **Summarizing; cloze exercise; process writing.** Have students write a summary of the poem using their graphic organizers. Follow the steps for process writing. You may want to save this page and students' writing in their **Assessment Portfolios.**

Answer the following questions about the poem "Africa Dream."

1. How did the girl cross the ocean? _____

2. Where did she land? _____

3. Where did she shop? _____

4. What did she ride on? _____

5. What kind of dance did she dance? _____

6. What kind of song did she sing? _____

7. What did she turn into? _____

QUICK WRITE
Write about your family, dreams, far-away lands.

_____

_____

_____

_____

_____

_____

_____

_____

_____

_____

_____

_____

_____

_____

_____

_____

_____

(Supports Student Book 2, pages 64–67) **Recalling details; creative writing.** Students work independently. Allow time for students to share their work with the class.

67

A. *Fill in the blanks with the correct forms of the verbs.*

I _____ I was an animal trainer. I _____ a great
     (dream)   (live)

life. I _____ across the country. I _____ in the best
        (travel)   (stay)

hotels. My fans _____ me. They _____ when the
                    (love)   (cheer)

lions _____ . They _____ when the tigers
         (dance)   (clap)

_____ through hoops. They _____ and
     (jump)   (whistle)

_____ their feet. It was a great dream!
     (stamp)

B. *Work with a partner. Say each word out loud. Listen carefully.
Does the ending sound like a -T or a -D? Write each word in the
correct column.*

	-T	-D
stopped		
baked		
talked		
walked		
cheered		
clapped		
thanked		
stayed		
lived		
loved		
danced		
jumped		
traveled		
watched		
washed		
pushed		

(Supports Student Book 2, page 68) **Choosing the right verb form; categorizing.** Students work independently to complete exercise A, then with partners to complete exercise B. Check answers in class.

Fill in the blanks with the correct forms of the verbs.

I _____ I was in English class. Principal Mason
    (dream)

_____ into the classroom. He _____ to me and
(come)   (point)

said, "Harold, you have to be the teacher." He _____ at the
                                     (look)

students and _____ them to be good. Then he
             (tell)

_____ out of the room. I _____ scared, but I
(walk)   (feel)

_____ to the front of the room. I _____ the
(walk)   (open)

teacher's desk and _____ some chalk. I _____
         (get)   (write)

some words on the board. I _____ to explain the exercise to
        (start)

the students. The students _____ and _____. I
       (talk)   (laugh)

_____ Principal Mason. He _____ the phone. Then
(call)   (answer)

I _____ up.
 (wake)

QUICK WRITE
Write for about five minutes about a dream of your own. Who was in your dream? What happened? Where did you go? How did you get there? What did you do there?

_____

_____

_____

_____

_____

_____

_____

(Supports Student Book 2, page 69) **Choosing the right verb form; creative writing.** Students work independently. Check answers in class. Encourage oral presentations.

69

The dream catcher didn't catch this nightmare. Sometimes things happen in dreams that could not happen in real life. Look at these scenes from a dream and write what's happening in each scene of the storyboard.

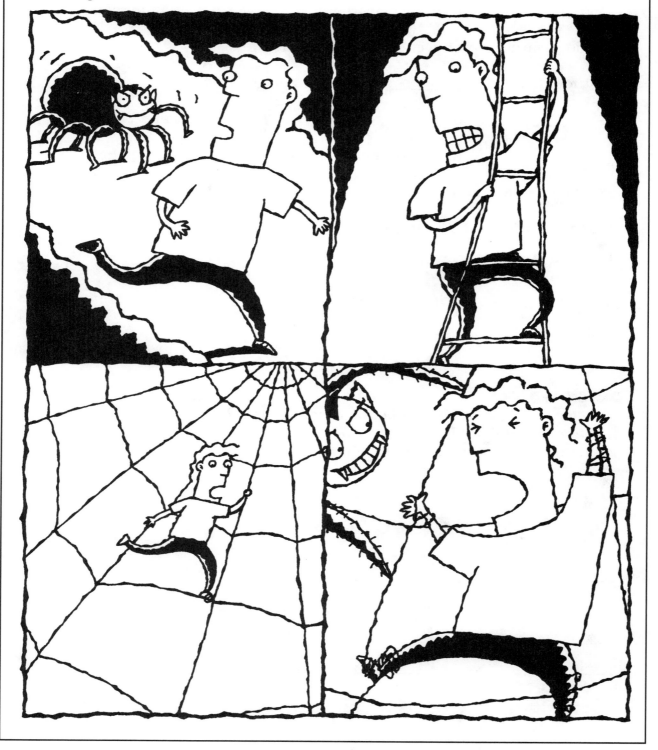

What happens next?

Now write about what happened in the dream.

_____

_____

_____

_____

_____

_____

_____

_____

_____

_____

_____

(Supports Student Book 2, pages 70–71) **Completing a storyboard; writing.** Students may work independently. Allow time for students to share their work with the class.

71

Complete the Venn Diagram about the National Dance Institute.

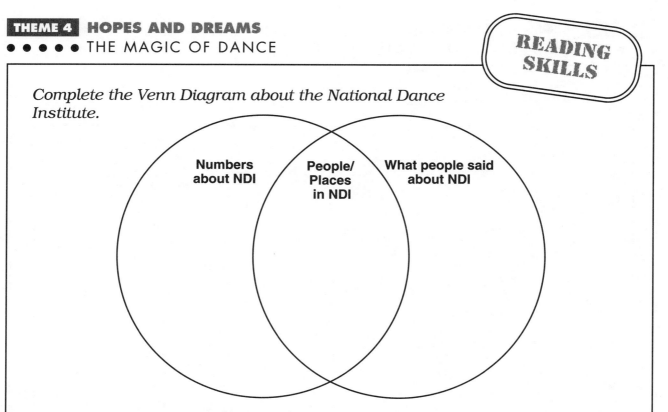

Numbers about NDI   **People/ Places in NDI**   **What people said about NDI**

A. *Read carefully. Mark the sentences true or false.*

1. _____ Jacques d'Amboise was a very famous singer.

2. _____ He was the main dancer for the New York City Ballet.

3. _____ Jacques became too old to perform.

4. _____ He became a baseball player.

5. _____ NDI means the New Dance Institute.

6. _____ NDI started in 1996.

7. _____ NDI was small in the beginning.

8. _____ The Event of the Year happens in July.

9. _____ More than 3,000 kids dance together.

10. _____ More than 80% of NDI dancers are talented.

11. _____ Some dancers are homeless.

12. _____ Some dancers are blind.

13. _____ Only some of the dancers love to dance.

14. _____ NDI dancers don't work together.

15. _____ NDI dancers feel proud.

(Supports Student Book 2, pages 72–74) **Reading comprehension; using a diagram to record information; distinguishing true-false statements.** Using their Venn Diagrams, have students write short profiles of the National Dance Institute. Follow process writing steps. You may want to include final copies in students' **Assessment Portfolios**.

Work with a partner. Create a new dance. Choose some music you both like. Then decide how to move to the music. How will you stand? What will you do with your arms? How fast will you move? What special moves will you do?

Name your dance. Describe the new dance. Illustrate the dance. Teach your dance to the class!

_____

(name of dance)

_____

_____

_____

DATA BANK

hop

jump

turn

wave your arms

slide

step

clap

twist

spin

snap your fingers

© Addison-Wesley Publishing Company

(Supports Student Book 2, pages 72–74) **Vocabulary development; creating a dance.** Consider videotaping student performances to share with other classes or with parents. Students can narrate their dance steps and teach others in a class presentation.

Feeling Proud

The dancers at the National Dance Institute feel proud about themselves. They work hard at their dancing. You can be proud of yourself by working hard at things you like to do.

A. *Complete the following chart to show all the good things you do at home and at school.*

Are you friendly, polite, helpful?
Do you always try your best?
Do you help people in your family or in your neighborhood?
Include these things in your chart.

At Home	At School	At Play

B. *Now that you know what a fantastic person you are, what are your goals? What do you want to do? What will help you feel proud of yourself?*

(Supports Student Book 2, pages 72–74) **Using a chart to record information; providing information about self.** Have students use their graphic organizers to write short compositions about their positive qualities. Follow process writing steps. You may want to include final copies in students' **Assessment Portfolios**.

A. *Read "I Have a Dream" again. Talk with your partner
about a dream you have for the world. What do you
hope life will be like for your children? Write a speech
about that dream. Read your speech to the class.*

_____
(poem title)

I have a dream

That one day this _____ will _____ up

And live out the _____ meaning of its creed;

"We _____ these _____ to be self-evident,

That all _____ are _____."

I have a dream

That one day on the _____ of _____

The _____ of former _____

And the _____ of _____

Will be able to _____ down _____

At the _____ of _____.

I have a dream

That my _____ little _____

Will one day _____ in a _____

Where _____ will not be _____

By the _____ of their _____

But by the _____ of their _____.

(Supports Student Book 2, page 75) **Cloze exercise.** Students complete the page independently. Allow time
for students to share their work with the class.

The Edison Reporter

Multicultural Festival Held at Edison School

The last week in October was multicultural week at the Edison School. During this week, we honored the many cultural backgrounds of the students in our school. In social studies classes, students made signs for the school lobby that said welcome in various languages. We had beautiful and colorful welcome banners in English, Arabic, Spanish, Vietnamese, Haitian Creole, Irish Gaelic, Chinese, Hebrew, and Swahili. During the festival, many parents and other family members visited the school. They brought family treasures that reflect their family's cultural background. Many families had two or more cultures to share.

On the final day of the festival, the whole school celebrated with a multicultural lunch provided by parents and several local ethnic restaurants. After lunch, a big show took place in the auditorium. Each class participated as a group. Individual students with special talents also performed. Everyone had a great time and people are already looking forward to next year's festival.

Fill in the name of your school below. Use the lines to write a first draft of an article for your school newspaper. Write about a recent event in your school or community.

The _____ Reporter

_____

_____

_____

_____

_____

_____

_____

_____

© Addison-Wesley Publishing Company

(Supports Student Book 2, pages 76–79) **Process writing; computer connection.** Students read the sample article, then write their own. If you have access to a computer and desktop publishing software, create a classroom/school newspaper. Students can contribute to the newspaper on a regular basis.

_____

_____

_____

_____

_____

_____

_____

_____

_____

_____

_____

_____

_____

_____

_____

_____

_____

_____

_____

_____

_____

_____

_____

_____

_____

(Supports Student Book 2, pages 76–79) **Process writing.** Have students follow the steps for process writing: Prewriting/Gathering Information, First Draft, Editing/Revising, Final Draft. They should use this page for their first drafts. Make sure students answer the five "W's" in their articles. You may want to save this page in students' **Assessment Portfolios.**

Read the letter from Sleepy Sue on page 79 of your student book. How can she get some sleep? Write a letter to Sleepy Sue.

Mail Box

_____

_____

_____

_____

_____

_____

_____

_____

_____

_____

_____

© Addison-Wesley Publishing Company

(Supports Student Book 2, pages 76–79) **Expressing opinions; letter writing; process writing.** Reread the Mailbox letter on page 78 of the student book with students. Discuss the topic. Ask students to give their advice in a reply letter. Follow the steps for process writing. You may want to save this page in students' **Assessment Portfolios.**

SCIENCE PROCESS SKILLS

CD ROM Science: Time Zones

IT'S 2:00 IN THE AFTERNOON, HERE IN ETHIOPIA. I WANT TO CALL MY FRIEND SARA IN NORTH AMERICA, BUT IT'S ONLY 4:00 IN THE MORNING THERE. I DON'T WANT TO WAKE HER. I'LL HAVE TO WAIT.

NOW, IT'S 6:00. I CAN CALL SARA BEFORE I HAVE DINNER. SHE SHOULD BE AWAKE BY NOW.

SARA, IT'S CD ROM. I'M IN ETHIOPIA. IT'S 6:00 IN THE EVENING, HERE. DID I WAKE YOU?

NO, IT'S 8:00 A.M. I'M JUST EATING BREAKFAST.

OH, GOOD. I'M GLAD I CAUGHT YOU BEFORE YOU LEFT FOR SCHOOL. HOW ARE YOU?

I'M FINE, AND I'M GLAD YOU CALLED! LET'S CALL SOMEONE IN JAPAN!

YOUR **T**URN   Draw conclusions. Talk about what people may be doing at that time in each place.

(Supports Student Book 2, pages 76–79) **Science process skills.** Consider videotaping the experiment to share with other classes or with parents. Use as a Language Experience Activity. Have students write about the activity either individually or as a class writing experience. You may want to include this writing in students' **Assessment Portfolios.**

SKILLS CHECK

VOCABULARY REVIEW
Circle the word in each group that does not belong. Tell why.

	A	B	C	D
1	cheer	clap	whistle	magic
2	amazing	dream	lonesome	long
3	perform	NDI	jump	dance
4	understood	dreamed	listen	danced
5	trainer	tiger	dancer	teacher
6	nation	country	land	United States
7	movie star	musician	software	dancer
8	building	athlete	Olympics	medal
9	camera	photographer	judge	film
10	Africa	village	marketplace	city

QUICK WRITE
Write about a career that interests you. Tell what a person in that career does all day.

_____

_____

_____

_____

_____

_____

_____

_____

_____

_____

(Supports Student Book 2, pages 80–81) **Assessment; reinforcing key vocabulary.** Work with students individually. Have students explain why they chose each word from the list. The explanation shows that the student has mastered the vocabulary. You may want to save this page in students' **Assessment Portfolios.**

HOW ARE YOU DOING?

Now I Can	yes	no	not sure
1. talk about careers.			
2. read a poem.			
3. use the past tense.			
4. read a non-fiction story.			
5. make a dream catcher.			
6. complete a Venn Diagram.			
7. create a dance.			
8. write a speech.			

Now I Know	In My Language	yes	no	not sure
cheer				
clap				
perform				
dream				
jump				
magic				
sleep				
dance				
travel				
whistle				
speech				
pride				
nation				
character				
judge				
marketplace				
Africa				
talent				

___ Teacher Check

(Supports Student Book 2, pages 80–81) **Self-assessment; Home-School connection.** Students work independently. Review the page with each student and check off your approval. Students can take a copy of this
page home to share with family members. You may want to save this page in students' **Assessment
Portfolios.**

When you dream a dream,
You can be someone else;
A sailor, a princess, or just stay yourself.

There are many kinds of dreams. Write and sing a verse of your own.

I dreamt I was a _____

_____

_____

_____

Draw a picture of your dream and tell about it.

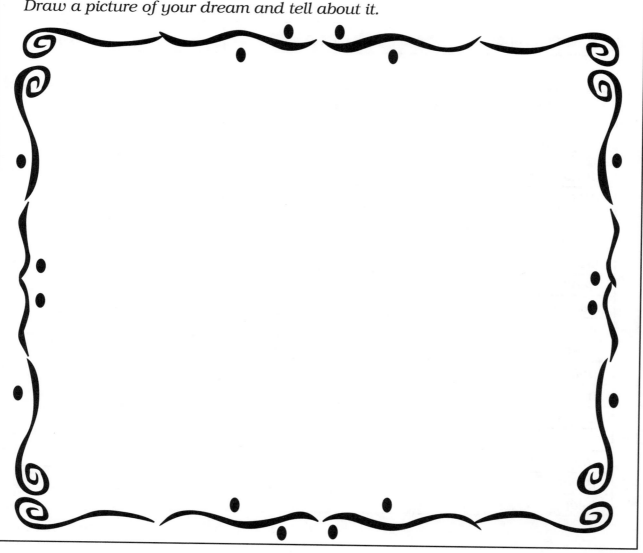

(Supports Student Book 2, page 82) **Creating an original song verse; learning language through song.** Students work independently. Volunteers may sing their new verses to the class.

Look at the pictures. Tell what you see. Write about the pictures.

Words I Already Know	New Words I Have Learned

(Supports Student Book 2, page 83) **Activating prior knowledge; self-assessment.** Students write the words they know before the lesson begins, then the words they have learned at the end of the lesson. You may want to save this page in students' **Assessment Portfolios.**

Complete the chart below with information from the story on pages 84–89 in your student book. Write who, what, when, where, what happened, and other important information from each part of the story in the boxes below.

The Job

_____
_____
_____
_____
_____

The Letter

_____
_____
_____
_____
_____

Together Again

_____
_____
_____
_____
_____

(Supports Student Book 2, pages 84–89) **Using a chart to record information; summarizing; process writing.** Have students write a summary of the story using their graphic organizers. Follow the steps for process writing. You may want to include this page and students' final summaries in their **Assessment Portfolios.**

READING SKILLS

How Do You Know?

Find the line in the story "The Family from Vietnam," that means the same as the words in each box. Write the exact words from the story in the box on the right.

Mai is homesick for Vietnam.	_____ _____ _____
Set was sad to see his family leave.	_____ _____ _____
Mai didn't hate her work.	_____ _____ _____
Set likes California.	_____ _____ _____
The children were doing well in America.	_____ _____ _____
Set wants to see his family soon.	_____ _____ _____

(Supports Student Book 2, pages 84–89) **Reading comprehension; using a chart to record information.**
Students may work individually or with partners. Check answers in class.

85

Complete the letter with the correct words.

Dear Mai, Dear Bao, Dear Thi,

I am alive and well. I read _____ ad in the Vietnamese

newspaper here in California. I was so _____ to see it!

My heart was never so _____ as the day I saw

your _____ fly away. I never stop _____ about

you. I was sent to _____ army base in California. Now I am

_____ with an American family. We must be together

_____. California is _____. But you are

_____ beautiful. I will come to you _____ soon as

I can. We _____ be together again soon.

My love,
Set

QUICK WRITE

*Imagine that you receive a letter from a family member that you
have not seen for a few years. Write a letter that tells how you
feel and what you have been doing over the past two or three
years.*

_____

_____

_____

_____

_____

_____

_____

_____

(Supports Student Book 2, pages 84–89) **Cloze exercise; writing.** Students work independently. Volunteers
may share their work with the class.

Strategies for Learning English

Mai's children learned English very quickly. Here are some of the ways they learned English.

They watched television.
They read books.
They talked with friends who speak English.
They listened to the radio.
They studied ESL.
They kept a notebook of new words.

A. *What are your strategies for learning English?*

At Home	At School	At Play

B. *Keep a diary about learning English for a week. Write down all the ways that you learn English each day. Write down new words you learn and where you learned them.*

(Supports Student Book 2, pages 84–89) **Using a chart to record information; note-taking; using learning strategies.** Discuss learning strategies with the class. Students complete the page independently. Volunteers may share their diaries at the end of the week. Discuss.

Hopes and Dreams

Set is now with Mai and the children. Think about each person in the family. What do you think each person wants? Write as many wishes and dreams as you can think of for each person in the story.

Set's hopes and dreams

_____

_____

_____

_____

_____

Mai's hopes and dreams

_____

_____

_____

_____

_____

Bao's and Thi's hopes and dreams

_____

_____

_____

_____

_____

(Supports Student Book 2, pages 84–89) **Using a chart to record information; creative writing.** Have students write a composition about the characters in the story. Encourage them to use their graphic organizers. Follow the steps for process writing. You may want to keep this assignment in students' **Assessment Portfolios.**

Have You Ever Cried?

A. *Read and practice the conversation between Bao and Thi.*

"Thi, have you ever cried at school?"

"No, Bao. I have never cried at school. I almost cried when I first came to our new school, but I didn't."

"Why did you almost cry?"

"I almost cried because I didn't know anyone in my class, and no one spoke to me. I felt so sad and lonely."

"But now you have lots of friends, don't you?"

"Yes, I have made some wonderful friends. I never feel like crying when I'm with them. I feel like laughing."

B. *Study the conversation above. Then, ask a partner the questions below. Take notes about your partner's answers. Ask follow-up questions such as: Why? Where? How did you feel? Did you like it? What was it like? What do you think now? Write a paragraph about your conversation.*

1. Have you ever flown on an airplane?
2. Have you ever met a movie star?
3. Have you ever swum in the Pacific Ocean?
4. Have you ever seen a football game?
5. Have you ever won a dance contest?
6. Have you ever forgotten your homework?
7. Have you ever moved to a new house and felt homesick?
8. Have you ever shopped at a mall?
9. Have you ever cooked a turkey dinner?
10. Have you ever lived in another country?

(Supports Student Book 2, pages 84–89) **Practicing conversations; note-taking; writing.** Students use the model conversation and the questions as springboards for more paired conversations to practice.

Read the story on pages 90-91 of your student book again. Then read the questions and answers below. Write the correct pronouns in the blanks. Use the data bank to help you.

DATA BANK

he/she	her/him/	they/them

1. How old is Elizabeth?

   _____ is 100 years old.

2. What did Elizabeth's father encourage her to do in World War I?

   _____ encouraged _____ to go to France and drive an ambulance.

3. Who did Elizabeth meet in France?

   _____ met _____ husband in France.

4. What did Elizabeth do for her husband?

   _____ drive _____ to the hospital.

5. What did Elizabeth's mother tell her?

   _____ mother told her _____ could be as smart as the boys.

6. What did Elizabeth do in 1919?

   _____ stood up for a woman's right to vote.

7. What did black and white people to as they listened to Dr. King's speech in 1963?

   _____ stood together and said _____ wanted to live peacefully.

8. How does Elizabeth feel about computers, VCRs, and bank machines?

   _____ thinks _____ are complicated.

   _____ can't keep up with _____.

9. What did people do when Elizabeth stopped talking?

   _____ clapped for _____.

(Supports Student Book 2, pages 90–91) **Pronouns.** Students can complete the page independently. Check answers in class.

Pronouns take the place of people and things in sentences. Find these sentences in the story on pages 90-91 of your student book. Next to each sentence, write the person or thing that the underlined pronoun refers to.

<u>She</u> was born in 1895 in Montgomery, Alabama.

_____

<u>He</u> was wounded and I drove him to the hospital.

_____

<u>We</u> stood in front of the white house.

_____

That was in 1919, and we weren't afraid to look right at President Wilson and say to <u>him</u>, 'Equal rights for women!'

_____

Black and white Americans stood together—more than two hundred thousand of <u>us</u>.

_____

<u>They</u> frightened you.

_____

I say to <u>myself</u>, Elizabeth, you have seen a man walk on the moon.

_____

<u>You</u> have seen a black man run for president of the United States.

_____

I can't keep up with <u>them</u>.

_____

When Grandma stopped talking, everyone clapped for <u>her</u>.

_____

(Supports Student Book 2, pages 90–91) **Antecedents.** Students can complete the page independently. Check answers in class.

91

Where Is It Made or Grown?

The map on the opposite page shows some of the products of the states in the United States. Use the map and its key to answer these questions.

1. In what two states are automobiles made?

   Automobiles are made in Michigan and Indiana.

2. In what states are oranges grown?

   _____

3. Where is corn grown?

   _____

4. Where are potatoes grown?

   _____

5. Where is oil found?

   _____

6. Where are cattle raised?

   _____

7. Where is sugar produced?

   _____

8. Where are dairy products made?

   _____

9. Where is cotton grown?

   _____

10. Where is wheat grown?

    _____

11. Where are peanuts grown?

    _____

MATH SKILLS

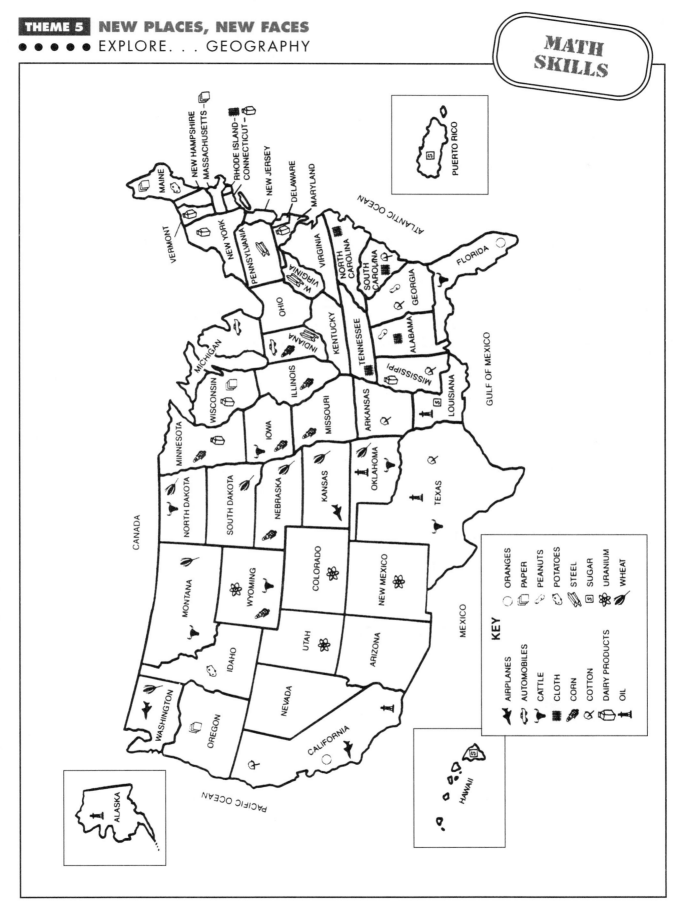

(Supports Student Book 2, pages 92–93) **Reading a map.** Students may work individually or with partners.
Check answers in class.

93

What Do You Think?

A. *Think about the poem on pages 94–95 in your student book.*
Use these questions to help you.

1. Did you like what the poem says? Why or why not?
2. What does "Sing of her beauty and greatness to-be" mean?
Who does *her* refer to?

B. *Talk to a partner about America. Choose some of these questions to talk*
about. Make notes about your conversation on the lines below.

1. What is your favorite part of nature? Why?
2. What are your neighbors like? How are they different?
How are they alike?
3. What words would you use to describe America?

_____

_____

_____

_____

_____

_____

_____

_____

_____

_____

_____

_____

_____

_____

(Supports Student Book 2, page 94) **Discussing emotions; note-taking.** Reread, or play the tape of, the poem on page 94 of the student book. Discuss the poem as a class. Then have students complete the page with partners.

Places and Faces

Fill in the chart with places and faces you see every day.

Things in the Country	Things in the City
Things in the Sky	**Expressions on People's Faces**

QUICK WRITE

Now write a paragraph about the places and faces you see every day. You can begin your paragraph with the words: I like to look at. . .

_____

_____

_____

_____

_____

(Supports Student Book 2, page 95) **Using a chart to record information; writing.** Have students use their graphic organizers to help them write a composition. Follow the steps for process writing. You may want to include final copies in students' **Assessment Portfolios**.

PROCESS WRITING

The Edison Reporter

Edison Students Sing at Local Nursing Home

The Edison School Chorus gave a concert for elderly patients at the Cedar Lane Nursing Home on Saturday, February 27. The forty-student chorus is directed by Ms. Ellen LeBlanc, Edison's music teacher.

The students arrived after lunch and sang to a full house in Cedar Lane's recreation room. The songs included popular U.S. hits as well as songs in several other languages. The seniors loved the show. After the show, the students visited with the patients. The Cedar Lane staff surprised both residents and singers with an ice cream party!

Many of the students said they will come back to visit on their own or in small groups. Mr. Cardoso, director of Cedar Lane, told our reporter, "Many of our patients have visitors only on the weekends. Some of them have no family to visit them. They get very lonely. Having young people visit them is a wonderful gift."

Amy Lee, a student in the seventh grade, says, "I had a lot of fun. Visiting the patients at Cedar Lane is great. My grandmother died last year and I really miss her. Visiting elderly people is like visiting my grandma. They love to hear about what's going on in my life and in the community. I'll definitely go back again."

● ●

Fill in the name of your school below. Use the lines to write a first draft of an article for your school newspaper. Write about something nice you've done for the community or something you would like to do.

The _____ Reporter

_____

_____

_____

_____

_____

_____

(Supports Student Book 2, pages 96–99) **Process writing; computer connection.** Students read the sample article, then write their own. If you have access to a computer and desktop publishing software, create a classroom/school newspaper. Students can contribute to the newspaper on a regular basis.

_____

_____

_____

_____

_____

_____

_____

_____

_____

_____

_____

_____

_____

_____

_____

_____

_____

_____

_____

_____

_____

_____

_____

_____

_____

_____

_____

_____

(Supports Student Book 2, pages 96–99) **Process writing.** Have students follow the steps for process writing: Prewriting/Gathering Information, First Draft, Editing/Revising, Final Draft. They should use this page for their first drafts. Make sure students answer the five "W's" in their articles. You may want to save this page in students' **Assessment Portfolios.**

Read the letter from Country Joe on page 99 of your student book. What should he do? Write a letter to Country Joe.

Mail Box

_____

_____

_____

_____

_____

_____

_____

_____

_____

_____

(Supports Student Book 2, pages 96–99) **Expressing opinions; letter writing; process writing.** Reread the Mailbox letter on page 98 of the student book with students. Discuss the topic. Ask students to give their advice in a reply letter. Follow the steps for process writing. You may want to save this page in students' **Assessment Portfolios.**

© Addison-Wesley Publishing Company

SCIENCE PROCESS SKILLS

CD ROM Science: Inertia

YOUR **T**URN   Try the inertia experiment. You'll need a cup, a coin, and an index card.

	Coins Landed in Cup	Coins Landed Outside of Cup
Trial 1		
Trial 2		
Trial 3		
Trial 4		
Trial 5		

Collect and record data. Work with a partner. Set your coins up all heads or all tails. Did they land the same way?

Draw conclusions. Compare your data with other students.

(Supports Student Book 2, pages 96–99) **Science process skills; comparing/contrasting.** Students work with partners to complete the chart. Consider videotaping the experiment to share with other classes or with parents. Use as a Language Experience Activity. Have students write about the activity either individually or as a class writing experience. You may want to include this writing in students' **Assessment Portfolios.**

SKILLS CHECK

VOCABULARY REVIEW

Circle the word in each group that does not belong. Tell why.

	A	B	C	D
1	Mai	Set	Lancaster	Bao
2	sad	happy	cry	down
3	prize	lose	medal	win
4	shave	head	face	floor
5	China	Japan	Puerto Rico	India
6	grouchy	confused	populous	frustrated
7	pretend	decide	feel	walk
8	string	beads	glue	spider
9	emotions	group	crowd	people
10	north	Asia	south	southwest

QUICK WRITE

Write about your first day at your new school. How did you feel?
Then write about how you feel today. What is different?

_____

_____

_____

_____

_____

_____

_____

_____

_____

_____

(Supports Student Book 2, pages 100–101) **Assessment; reinforcing key vocabulary.** Work with students individually. Have students explain why they chose each word from the list. The explanation shows that the student has mastered the vocabulary. You may want to save this page in students' **Assessment Portfolios.**

HOW ARE YOU DOING?

Now I Can	yes	no	not sure
1. complete a graphic organizer.			
2. explain the term inertia.			
3. find specific information in a story.			
4. gather data for an experiment.			
5. identify several Asian countries.			
6. make a bead necklace.			
7. use strategies for learning English.			

Now I Know	In My Language	yes	no	not sure
separate				
application				
missing				
village				
spider				
web				
crowd				
announce				
grouchy				
confused				
frustrated				
populous				
regions				
locate				
shave				
wrestling				
string				
beads				
pretend				
emotions				

___ Teacher Check

(Supports Student Book 2, pages 100–101) **Self-assessment; Home-School connection.** Students work independently. Review the page with each student and check off your approval. Students can take a copy of this page home to share with family members. You may want to save this page in students' **Assessment Portfolios.**

Sing the song "Feelings and Emotions." Then fill in the blanks below.

It makes me _____ when _____ singing
    with my friends,
Talk about feelings, talk about emotions.

Oh, _____ happy, want to _____ it
    again and again,
Talk about feelings, talk about emotions.

It makes me _____ when my mama picks _____
    me,
Talk about feelings, talk about emotions.

Oh, so angry, I _____ to climb a _____,
Talk about feelings, talk about emotions.

It makes me sad _____ my friends _____
    go away,
Talk about feelings, talk about emotions.

Oh, so _____, I wish that they _____ stay,
Talk about feelings, talk about emotions.

It makes _____ shy when I'm in a _____ place,
Talk about feelings, talk about emotions.

Oh, so _____, I want to hide _____ face,
Talk about feelings, talk about emotions.

(Supports Student Book 2, page 102) **Cloze exercise; learning language through song.** Students complete the page independently. Volunteers may share their work with the class.

Look at the picture. Tell what you see. Write about the picture.

Her name is Eggy
She weighs
130 pounds

Animal: Hampsters
Name. Rosie, Susie
and Chicuito

His name is Lollipop.
He knows 50 words.

Words I Already Know	**New Words I Have Learned**

(Supports Student Book 2, page 103) **Activating prior knowledge; self-assessment.** Students write the
words they know before the lesson begins, then the words they have learned at the end of the lesson. You may
want to save this page in students' **Assessment Portfolios.**

Hooves and Horns

*Animal body parts are different from human body parts. Look at
the illustrations to learn some of these important words.*

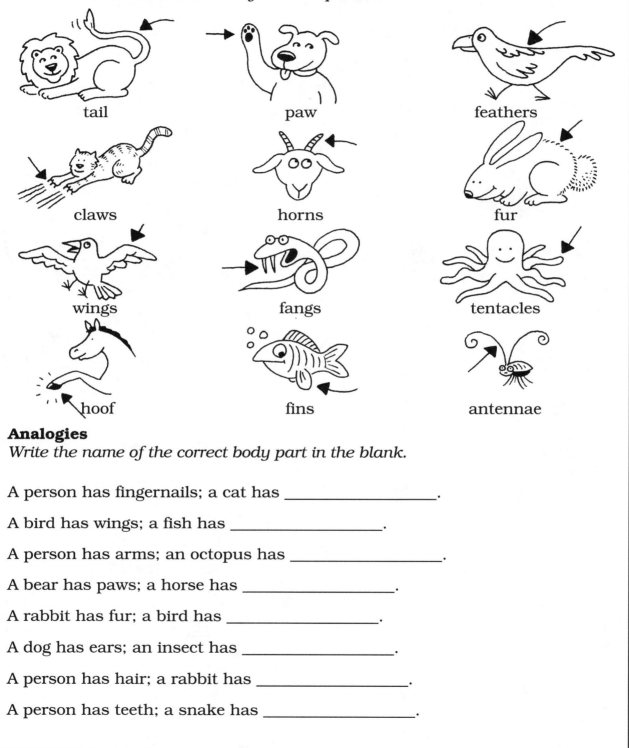

tail   paw   feathers

claws   horns   fur

wings   fangs   tentacles

hoof   fins   antennae

Analogies
Write the name of the correct body part in the blank.

A person has fingernails; a cat has _____.

A bird has wings; a fish has _____.

A person has arms; an octopus has _____.

A bear has paws; a horse has _____.

A rabbit has fur; a bird has _____.

A dog has ears; an insect has _____.

A person has hair; a rabbit has _____.

A person has teeth; a snake has _____.

DATA COLLECTION

Write the names of animals that fit into each category.
Use the word bank and your own words.

Animals with fur	Animals with tails	Animals with claws

Animals with wings	Animals with hooves	Animals with horns

WORD BANK

goat cow horse buffalo

parrot parakeet eagle goldfish

koala fly mouse jaguar

zebra manatee alligator quetzal

kangaroo elephant bat mosquito

Fill in the chart below with information from "Animals in Danger."

Name of Animal	From Where?	Dangers	What Can Be Done?
Elephant	Africa	killed for its tusks	Pass laws against hunting it.

Use the information in the chart to decide if the following sentences are true or false.

_____ Elephants are not in danger because there are so many of them.

_____ The macaws cannot find nuts from the trees to eat because farmers have cut down the trees.

_____ The chimpanzees are often sold to zoos and to people who want them as pets.

_____ The pandas have no trouble finding food and shelter.

_____ The quetzal is often killed for its beautiful feathers.

(Supports Student Book 2, pages 104–107) **Using a chart to record information; distinguishing true-false statements.** Students complete the page independently. Check answers in class. Students can write compositions about endangered animals using their graphic organizers. Follow the steps for process writing.

Find the line in "Animals in Danger" that means the same as the following sentences. Write it below.

1. People pay a lot of money for macaws.

_____

_____

_____

2. Some people and zoos like to buy chimpanzees.

_____

_____

_____

3. There isn't enough food for the giant panda of China.

_____

_____

_____

4. Farmers shoot wolves.

_____

_____

_____

5. The jaguar is homeless.

_____

_____

_____

6. Elephants are often killed for just one part of their body.

_____

_____

_____

(Supports Student Book 2, pages 104–107) **Reading comprehension.** Students may work individually or with partners. Check answers in class.

107

A. *Match the columns to explain what will happen in each weather situation.*

1. If it rains _____   a. we'll go to the beach.

2. If it snows _____   b. we will eat dinner on the porch.

3. If it thunders _____   c. I'll wear my jacket.

4. If it's windy _____   d. we'll build a snowman.

5. If it's cold _____   e. I'll use my new umbrella.

6. If it's foggy _____   f. we'll shut the windows.

7. If it's hot _____   g. the dog will hide under the bed.

8. If it's warm _____   h. the pilot won't fly the plane.

Work with a partner to compare your answers. Read your complete sentences to each other.

B. *Now make up your own "what if" sentences. Write what will happen in each sentence below.*

1. If Tom has a party _____

2. If the television is too loud _____

3. If Bill feels sick _____

4. If Jeanette is hungry _____

5. If Martina wants to play basketball _____

6. If Mrs. Yu needs milk _____

7. If Henry wants a ride home from school _____

8. If Tasha saves $100 _____

After you complete your sentences, work with a partner to compare your answers. Read your complete sentences to each other.

(Supports Student Book 2, pages 108–109) **Present conditional tense; comparing.** Students complete exercises A and B independently. Check answers in class. Allow time for students to compare answers with a partner and read their complete sentences to each other.

Weather Emergencies

A. *There are different ways to respond to weather emergencies. It's very important to stay calm in any emergency and to be prepared. Read the following table to find out what to do during severe weather.*

Hurricane	listen to weather reports, evacuate, go down to the basement
Blizzard	buy extra groceries, get a flashlight and batteries
Drought	conserve water, take quick showers
Tornado	listen to weather reports, go down to the basement
Flood	listen to weather reports, move to high ground

B. *Now answer the following questions. Work with a partner.*

1. What will you do if a hurricane comes to your city or town?

_____

2. What will you do if you hear a tornado warning?

_____

3. What will you do if you hear a blizzard is coming?

_____

4. What will you do if there is a flood in your area?

_____

5. What will you do if there is a drought?

_____

Deserts

Deserts are very dry areas of land. There are deserts in North and South America, Africa, Asia, and Australia. About 30% of the total of Earth's land is desert. Some deserts are very dry. They get less than 10 inches of water per year. Other deserts are not so dry. They can get up to 20 inches of rain in a year.

Most people think that deserts are hot, dry, and lifeless places. Deserts can be hot and dry, but they are not lifeless. There are plants and animals who make their homes in the desert. These plants and animals have learned to survive the heat and the lack of rain.

The cactus plant is a familiar desert plant. It can survive in the desert because it stores water for future use. Whenever there is rain, the cactus roots soak up as much water as possible. The cactus stores and uses this water until the next rainfall. Mesquite, another desert plant, has long roots that travel up to 100 feet underground in search of water that is deep under the surface of the desert.

There are animals that also live in the desert. Many small desert animals like the kangaroo rat, the pack rat, and the pocket mouse, stay underground during the hot day. They come out at night to look for food. Reptiles, like snakes and lizards, use desert plants for shade to keep them cool during the hot days.

Answer the following questions about deserts.

1. What is a desert?
2. Where are the Earth's deserts located?
3. How much of the Earth's land is desert?
4. Are all deserts the same?
5. Can plants and animals live in the desert?
6. How does the cactus plant survive in the desert?
7. How does the mesquite plant survive in the desert?
8. Name some animals that live in the desert.
9. Where do small desert animals stay during the day?
10. How do reptiles stay cool?

(Supports Student Book 2, pages 110–111) **Reading comprehension; vocabulary development.** Students complete the page independently. Check answers in class.

Deserts and Rain Forests

A. *Complete the Venn Diagram to show how rain forests and deserts are similar and different. Use the readings on pages 110 and 111 of your student book and page 110 in your skills journal to find the information you need.*

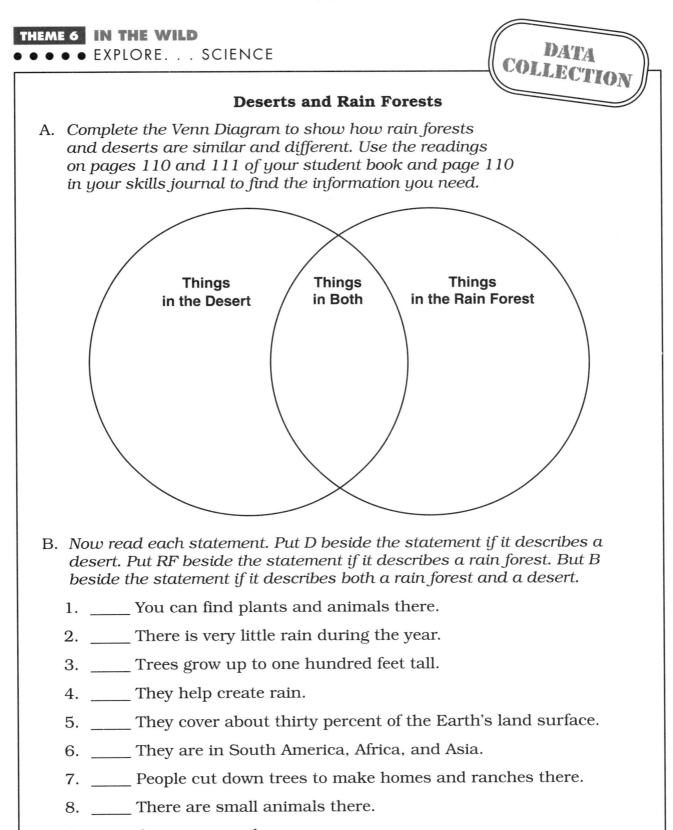

Things in the Desert   Things in Both   Things in the Rain Forest

B. *Now read each statement. Put D beside the statement if it describes a desert. Put RF beside the statement if it describes a rain forest. But B beside the statement if it describes both a rain forest and a desert.*

1. _____ You can find plants and animals there.

2. _____ There is very little rain during the year.

3. _____ Trees grow up to one hundred feet tall.

4. _____ They help create rain.

5. _____ They cover about thirty percent of the Earth's land surface.

6. _____ They are in South America, Africa, and Asia.

7. _____ People cut down trees to make homes and ranches there.

8. _____ There are small animals there.

9. _____ Cactus grows there.

10. _____ They receive over sixty inches of rain per year.

(Supports Student Book 2, pages 110–111) **Research; classifying.** Reread, or play the tape of, pages 110 and 111 of the student book. Then have students complete the page independently. Encourage students to find out more about this subject. Check answers in class.

Place the letter of the correct answer in the blank. Some answers may be used more than once.

1. They were often killed by speedboats. _____

2. They live in Australia. _____

3. Their home was taken away by swimmers. _____

4. They like to be petted. _____

5. People build houses for them. _____

6. Hunters kill them for their fur. _____

7. They are coming back to North America. _____

8. There are laws against killing this giant animal. _____

a. koalas
b. bluebirds
c. humpback whales
d. loggerhead turtles
e. manatees

How are the animals below being saved from extinction? Write a sentence or two for each.

1. the koala

_____

_____

2. bluebirds

_____

_____

3. the humpback whale

_____

_____

4. the loggerhead turtle

_____

_____

(Supports Student Book 2, pages 112–114) **Reading comprehension; writing.** Students complete the page independently. Check answers in class.

DATA COLLECTION

Choose one of the animals in "Animal Rescue Success Stories" and learn more about it. Ask a teacher or librarian to help you. Fill in the chart organizer below to help you get ready to write about your animal.

What does the animal look like?	What does the animal eat?	Where does it make its home (tree, cave, etc.)
Where does it live in the world?	How does it care for its babies?	Other interesting facts

QUICK WRITE

Now write about your animal. Start your first draft here. Then read your composition to a partner. Make corrections. Read it to a small group. Ask other people for suggestions. Talk to your teacher before beginning your final draft for your portfolio.

_____

_____

_____

_____

_____

_____

(Supports Student Book 2, pages 112–114) **Research; using a chart to record information; writing.** Help students research their chosen animals. Then have students complete the page independently. Volunteers may share their work with the class.

Ways to Help

What things or actions are helping wild animals to survive?
Put a check in front of them.

_____ Pollution.

_____ Planting trees in the forest.

_____ Hunting for sport or food.

_____ Taking wild animals for pets.

_____ Selling the horns, skins, fur, feathers of wild animals.

_____ Cutting up plastic rings.

_____ Building bird houses.

_____ Cutting down trees.

_____ Collecting wild birds.

_____ Recycling.

_____ Walking or biking instead of driving a car.

_____ Keeping some land especially for animals (nature preserves).

What Can We Do?

Talk to a classmate about what we can do about these problems.
Write down your ideas for each one.

air pollution _____

_____

water pollution _____

_____

too many people _____

_____

loss of rain forests _____

_____

hunting of wild animals _____

_____

(Supports Student Book 2, pages 112–114) **Reading comprehension; brainstorming; note-taking.** Students complete the top exercise independently. Then work with a partner to complete the bottom exercise. Check answers in class.

My Favorite Place in Nature

Think about a place in nature that you love. What can you see, feel, hear, touch, taste, and smell in that place? Write your answers in the chart.

Things I can touch	Things I can see	Things I can hear
Things I can smell	Things I can taste	Things I can feel

Write your own poem about your favorite place. Use the poem "In My Mountains" as a guide. Use the chart to help you think about your special place before you write your poem.

_____

_____

_____

_____

_____

_____

(Supports Student Book 2, page 115) **Brainstorming; using a chart to record information; writing.**
Students work independently, using their graphic organizers to help them write their poems. Volunteers may share their work with the class.

PROCESS WRITING

The Edison Reporter

Edison Holds Annual Pet Show

Edison School held its annual pet show on Saturday, June 6. Students and teachers brought their pets to the school yard at 10 a.m. Tables for goldfish, hamsters, snakes, and other animals in cages were set up in the shade. Each animal's container or collar held a card with the pet's name, animal category, age, and owner's name and grade. Students brought their cats in carriers and their dogs on leashes. It was very noisy and several dogs broke away from their owners and ran wild. Ms. Hernandez, our principal, looked very stressed, but she hurried along with the judging. Each student talked about his or her pet for a few minutes. The judges, Dr. Walker and Dr. Chow, our local veterinarians, asked the students questions about how they care for their pets. Prizes were given based on the health and appearance of the pet and on how the owners answered the pet care questions.

●●●●●●●●●●●●●●●●●●●●●●●●●●●●●●●●●●●●●●

Fill in the name of your school below. Use the lines to write a first draft of an article for your school newspaper. Write about your pet, a friend's pet, or a pet you'd like to have.

The _____ Reporter

_____

_____

_____

_____

_____

_____

_____

_____

© Addison-Wesley Publishing Company

(Supports Student Book 2, pages 116-119) **Process writing; computer connection.** Students read the sample article, then write their own. If you have access to a computer and desktop publishing software, create a classroom/school newspaper. Students can contribute to the newspaper on a regular basis.

PROCESS WRITING

(Supports Student Book 2, pages 116-119) **Process writing.** Have students follow the steps for process writing: Prewriting/Gathering Information, First Draft, Editing/Revising, Final Draft. They should use this page for their first drafts. Make sure students answer the five "W's" in their articles. You may want to save this page in students' **Assessment Portfolios.**

*Read the letter from Worried in Dallas on page 119 of your
student book. Write a letter explaining whether you agree or disagree
with Worried's friends.*

© Addison-Wesley Publishing Company

(Supports Student Book 2, pages 116–119) **Expressing opinions; letter writing; process writing.** Reread the
Mailbox letter on page 118 of the student book with students. Discuss the topic. Ask students to give their
advice in a reply letter. Follow the steps for process writing. You may want to save this page in students'
Assessment Portfolios.

CD Rom Science: Animal Tracks

YOUR TURN   Draw conclusions. Work with a partner to figure out what happened to the animals in the story. What made the different tracks? Make your own animal track story.

(Supports Student Book 2, pages 116–119) **Science process skills.** Consider videotaping the experiment to share with other classes or with parents. Use as a Language Experience Activity. Have students write about the activity either individually or as a class writing experience. You may want to include this writing in students' **Assessment Portfolios.**

SKILLS CHECK

VOCABULARY REVIEW

Circle the word in each group that does not belong. Tell why.

	A	B	C	D
1	bird	feathers	macaw	fur
2	jaguar	cat	wolf	tiger
3	paw	hoof	fur	foot
4	flood	tornado	pollution	blizzard
5	clouds	breeze	rain	water
6	protect	help	destroy	save
7	koala	manatee	humpback whale	rabbit
8	roam	swim	creep	sound
9	trash	recycle	pollution	garbage
10	nuts	bamboo	manatee	eucalyptus

QUICK WRITE

_____

_____

_____

_____

_____

_____

_____

_____

_____

_____

(Supports Student Book 2, page 120) **Assessment; reinforcing key vocabulary.** Work with students individually. Have students explain why they chose each word from the list. The explanation shows that the student has mastered the vocabulary. You may want to save this page in students' **Assessment Portfolios.**

HOW ARE YOU DOING?

Now I Can	yes	no	not sure
1. complete an analogy.			
2. react to weather emergencies.			
3. identify the five senses.			
4. identify animal body parts.			
5. help protect the environment.			
6. interpret a pie chart.			
7. talk about deserts.			

Now I Know	In My Language	yes	no	not sure
disappear				
extinct				
feathers				
fur				
tail				
paw				
claw				
hoof				
horn				
wild				
collect				
flood				
drought				
foggy				
lightning				
tornado				
blizzard				
pollution				
stream				
breeze				

___ Teacher Check

(Supports Student Book 2, page 121) **Self-assessment; Home-School connection.** Students work independently. Review the page with each student and check off your approval. Students can take a copy of this page home to share with family members. You may want to save this page in students' **Assessment Portfolios.**

Make up a dance for the song "Listen to the Water."
Use arm motions to act out "listen" and "rolling."

Flap your arms like birds for the first verse.

Pretend you are swimming like fish for the second verse.

What else do you see by the waterside?
Make up more verses and motions for this song.

We saw some _____ by the waterside.

We saw some _____ by the waterside.

We saw some _____ by the waterside.

Oh, oh by the waterside.

Oh, oh by the waterside.

(Supports Student Book 2, page 122) **Creating an original song verse.** Students may work in pairs, small groups, or as a class. Plan a class presentation of the new verses and motions.